Lenor Madruga Chappell

Women *of a*
Certain Age

Barringer Publishing, Naples, Florida
www.barringerpublishing.com

Design and layout by Linda S. Duider

ISBN 978-1-954396-03-6

Library of Congress Cataloging-in-Publication Data

Printed in U.S.A.

Women of a Certain Age
Lenor Madruga Chappell

To Roix Chappell who always encourages me to take that next step . . .

Freedom

"Women of a Certain Age captures the essence of eleven sagacious ladies . . . and the magic of Lenor's improbable life . . ."

~ *Lucia Smith*

LENOR MADRUGA CHAPPELL

Table of Contents

Acknowledgments

I have to start by thanking my incredible husband, Roix Chappell, for his guidance in the sequences that required piloting expertise, and for his patience during the process of writing this book. How I love this man!

To the courageous and wise ladies who contributed their most intimate stories for this project. Without them this book would not exist. I thank you all.

To Susan O'Leary, my primary editor and dear friend who braved through hours and days not only editing and assisting with rewrites, but contributing her own remarkable essays. She is currently writing a novel titled *The Mercy Seat.*

To Diane Harris, my sister, my best friend, and biggest fan who hesitated when first asked to contribute to this book saying she didn't feel qualified. But, when I gave her a sisterly little push, knowing she had interesting experiences to share, she came through by writing a startling narrative.

To Lou Ann Hardister, a dear friend for over forty years, who, with no writing experience, wrote a compelling narrative filled with personal truths, humor and faith.

To Melinda Haldeman, my San Diego hostess and dear friend, for writing a breathtaking narrative while working on her own book, titled A Strange Angel, What my addicted daughter taught me about life and love.

To Cathy Zupan, my traveling buddy for many years, is a giver and a caretaker to family, friend or foe. Even with her many pursuits, she found the time to lend her engaging voice to this book. She, too, is working on a book, Joy of Life, a heart-warming narrative from a dog's perspective . . . and Joy has a lot to say!

Thank you Cynthia Zvanet Hovey for an amusing, provocative take on what it is really like to be a woman of a certain age.

To Sharon Carter. It didn't take a lot of persuasion for Sharon to write a piece on being a woman of a certain age and the wisdom that comes with it. My sincerest thanks for her contribution and for always believing in me.

To Sharon Boucher, my buddy in Costa Rica, who we learn from her lively narrative is not only a "Diva" in the theater but also a Diva in real life.

To Judith (J.J.) Thank you for your spiritual guidance, and offering just what was needed for women of a certain age to glean hope and inspiration through unconditional love.

To Shelley Charlesworth. When we met, I was struck by her profound philosophy about grieving. I asked if she'd like to share her experience with our readers and she did with extraordinary generosity.

To Diana Coogle who brought beautiful poetry and incomparable life adventures to this book.

To Ernest Brawley, author, brother, confidant, who was the first person to say, after my amputation, "You ought to write a book about your life." I responded, "Let me live it first! Since then, he has guided me through the writing of three books.

To Victoria Livingstone, my niece, who graciously devoted time and effort with suggestions for this book during the time she was completing, *One Step At A Time,* a screenplay based on my first book.

To Amy Belkin, who read the early rendition of this manuscript and gave me the "thumbs up!"

To Amy Ecenbarger for coming up with an evocative cover design that I had envisioned for *Women of a Certain Age.*

To my daughter: Christianna Madruga and Daniella Crowder for their unwavering and valuable support throughout the writing of this book. And to my grandchildren: Elliott Crowder (Golden Boy); Allie Poling (Beauty Queen); and Summer Poling (Cleopatra) for their cheeky humor that always keeps Grandma in her place.

To my publisher, Jeff Schlesinger for his faith and kind guidance during the writing of this book.

To Lucia Smith who brought her editing talent to some of my earlier stories.

To Cheryl Kopic for the laughter and joy while assisting with the back cover photo.

Introduction

"I'm not old I'm perennial."

~ Jane Fonda

I have always relished life and never considered aging something to fear. I had dealt with cancer and the amputation of my left leg and a part of my pelvis at the age of thirty-two. I had paid my dues, I figured, and it would take a lot more to bring me down than turning seventy. Or would it?

I decided I would not be a victim but star in this my third act. I will not just survive my coming years, I will thrive. However, with this choice, one question kept rearing its head; can I manage the demands of aging while sustaining the same upbeat attitude that's kept me motivated throughout these many years?

I wondered about other women of a certain age and what paths they've taken and how they're managing their own changing tides. So, I invited ordinary women with extraordinary stories to get real about aging—to talk honestly about how they're dealing with their own fears and what they've learned about living through them. With wit, humor and staunch frankness, these women explain, discuss, call out and examine what aging now means to them and how they have negotiated, and continue to negotiate, the dynamic currents of aging. Their experiences are classic and engaging and their individual voices distinct and rich. And, they dish out what they wish "someone" had told them about the process.

Cynthia gave up home and career late in life to become a charter captain for Mega Yachts. She shares her thoughts on aging which, notably, didn't stop her from writing a book, *There's a Yacht More to Life,* which was published in 2019.

Lou Ann (L.A.) was a hairdresser until she decided to follow her dream and design leather clothing under her own brand, 'Chic Skins,' for country stars and exclusive boutiques.

Sharon B. is a successful theater director, actor, and vocal coach who recently survived breast cancer and tells us why she feels "lucky."

Susan says she's sometimes charged up and ready to chase her dreams. Other days she just wishes someone would bring her a cup of tea or a glass of wine and let her be.

J.J. is a Spiritual Being . . . Having a Human Experience . . . Evolving her Consciousness . . . So she can Live in Joy . . . and Spread the Light.

Sharon C. enlightens on the idea that every age has its ups and downs. "Our age is just the current lens we are looking through. Focus on the moment and don't dwell in the past or the future."

Diana C. is a writer who has lived in Oregon's Siskiyou Mountains for half a century. She earned a Ph.D. in English one month before her sixty-eighth birthday. She married, for the first time, at the age of seventy-four, and lost her husband to cancer eleven months later.

Melinda. Friends kept asking Melinda how she felt about turning sixty. Her glib response was, "I'm okay with it." It had never bothered her until one day she felt "something unnamable" and realized that she was suddenly old.

Cathy asks the question "What is happiness? I'm happy today and I was in the past and I probably will be happy in the future. Let me tell you how I came to think this way."

Diane H. is a horse woman, rancher, artist and red-headed bombshell. At eighty years old, she's living the dream of a lifetime.

Shelley. "Don't cry because it's over, smile because it happened." That was something someone said to Shelley after she lost her husband. "Indeed," she thought, "but getting to that place takes some work."

In my response to aging, I've written personal stories and anecdotes of my own discoveries. Some are serious, inspirational, illuminating. Others are outrageous, foolish, awkward and funny. Our stories, together, powerfully impart what it means to possess a certain wisdom, a certain comfort, a certain sensuality, a certain persona . . . not despite but *precisely* because of the experience of growing older.

Women of a Certain Age was conceived as a project where mature women could share their experiences, but it also turned out to be a road map, or compass, for younger women as well, to inspire them to view aging not as an ending, but as a transformation. This book strives to be a multi-generational conduit for the empowering yet simple message that "aging" is just more living!

Chapter One

Aging is Just More Living

*"We are all lost to change, for no man can
know triumph unless he has known disaster,
or recognize joy without knowing grief, or
treasure health without having felt agony."*

~ Ernest K. Mann

I'm convinced that the past can teach us about the future.
I had no idea where my life would lead me each time that I
thought it was over . . . cancer, amputation, divorce, financial
struggles. I understand we all have setbacks and they can halt
us in our tracks. But, for some reason I've persevered. Perhaps,
it's because I was blessed with two second chances—a life after

cancer and a magical, new love after my husband left me for another woman.

The choices I've made over the past years, negotiating the hard and soft edges of life, confronting and overcoming this new experience of aging, have led me to this my seventy-ninth year.

I grew up in a large, supportive family during the '50s, attended San Francisco State on a drama scholarship, hitch-hiked though Europe in the early '60s, lived in Rome and worked dubbing Italian movies into English.

True love colored my life when I married my high school sweetheart and moved to a dairy farm near Tracy, California, in the heart of the San Joaquin valley. I loved farm life. I felt useful riding my horse out to the fields toting lunch to our workers, driving a tractor and baling hay alongside my husband. Life was good until the unthinkable occurred.

It was the morning of my thirty-second birthday, March 22, 1974. I lay on a steel gurney in a hospital corridor at the Mayo Clinic in Rochester, Minnesota, waiting to be wheeled into surgery. This was not to be an ordinary operation, but catastrophic—the amputation of my left leg and a part of my pelvis.

Quivering on the cold metal, I prayed for more time. Time to raise my two little girls, Christianna and Daniella. Time to share with my husband, Joseph. Time to live out my life.

Today, I'm cancer free. The life-threatening disease that visited me with such a vengeance has never returned. I've had the privilege of watching my girls grow into womanhood and to hear the small voices of my grandchildren. I've lived a life, like most women of a certain age, filtered with darkness and happiness. But for the most part, I've enjoyed purpose, passion and, unexpectedly, a new career as a writer.

I never expected, *One Step at a Time,* about the struggle to walk again after losing my leg to cancer, to hit the best-seller lists. I never imagined my picture would be on the covers of magazines or that I'd be interviewed on radio and television or featured at book signings throughout America and Europe. *One Step at a Time* ends with a kind of romantic "And they lived happily ever after" notion, but life sometimes just doesn't work out that way.

Two years after my first book's publication, tragedy moved into my life once again when I discovered my husband with another woman. Betrayal is a harsh word. The act is worse.

I had been so caught up in my own life, traveling and publicizing my book, that I hadn't noticed the gossip, or my husband's growing distance. Certainly, the public attention had turned my head, but I believed I could still have the best of both worlds as a farm wife and an author.

Sadly, my success was more than my husband could cope with. He felt slighted, somehow diminished, and began to drink heavily. Two years after the publication of my first book, he left.

Losing my husband was worse than losing my leg.

Suffering from the disgrace, and the ugly reality of my husband's disloyalty, I fled. Cramming my two little girls into my sports car. I left the ranch and everything I knew behind, heading for an unknown future in Southern California. Once settled in there, I began work on my second book.

In *The Next Leg of My Journey*, I confessed to some of the hidden aspects of my life after the surgery: pain, drug addiction, heartbreak and loss. I divulged all the intimate and excruciating details of the death of my marriage. And finally, I wrote of an exciting, new love that brought happiness, and high-altitude adventure into my world.

Daniella, my daughter, came home one day from the beach with a new friend who looked at me and said, "You ought to meet my Dad."

"Yeah?" I winked at Daniella, knowing her mom loves cowboys.

"Does he wear cowboy boots?"

"Yes, and he flies his own plane."

"Well, tell me him to come on over!"

Several years out of practice, I fell in love with Roix Chappell, a tall, dark and handsome French-Canadian. I was in my late forties, an amputee with two children and a pile of debts. But to Roix, all the baggage didn't matter. We married a year later and began an adventurous life together.

Roix, a private pilot for over forty years, has logged 4,000 hours in his small plane. The instant I met him, I knew I wanted to be with him. So, with steely determination, I sucked in my terrible fear of flying and over the last three decades have logged over 1700 hours of flight time riding shotgun alongside my husband.

Through the years, I've learned to remain calm and trust Roix even during spine-tingling flights like flying the twenty-six miles from Catalina Island to the mainland in pea-soup fog, being knocked on our side in severe turbulence over Donner Lake in the Sierra Nevada Mountains, meeting farmers in fields where we were forced to land, soaring past Yosemite's Half Dome and Mount Whitney, finding our way over Death Valley in the moonlight, and bedding under the wing while looking up at the stars, anticipating the next day's exploits—there's no better way to dream.

Today, the limitless sky is where I feel most happy and most free. It's where I forget about my disability and my age. It is up there where my perspective on the world shifts to match God's view of the horizon and the expanse below. Instead of fearing what lies ahead, I cherish the fact that aging is just more living.

Chapter Two

Face in the Mirror

"People are like stained-glass windows. They sparkle and shine when the sun is out, but when the darkness sets in, their true beauty is revealed only if there is a light from within."

~ Elizabeth Kubler-Ross

We women of a certain age, all have issues about our appearance. Personally, I'm more aware of my body because at a young age my body changed radically and forever.. When I look in the mirror, it's not my face I scrutinize, but the left side of my body and the shock of what I'm missing never diminishes. Nevertheless, I do not bemoan what I see in the mirror but feel grateful for the part of me that remains, the part I keep physically fit and in good working order!

When I go out, I camouflage my missing leg with appropriate clothes to hide my bulky prosthetic limb and appear more attractive and normal—not disabled. I camouflage the missing leg with suitable garments to hide the bulky prosthetic limb. Or when I'm not wearing the leg, I choose long dresses. I feel that there is no need to shock or embarrass people by an empty pant leg or a short skirt exposing the fact that I have only one leg.

This works for me. Often, when I walk into a room limping, people ask, "What happen to your foot?"

"What foot?" I respond with a grin.

However, when I don a bathing suit, it's pretty obvious that I'm an amputee. But because I love to swim and do often, be it an ocean, lake, river or pool, I do not hide my situation because I so desperately need to have a dip.

What we look like, and what we project, can be two different things. For example, a few years ago, Roix and I were on holiday in Costa Rica. Before even settling into our hotel room, we grabbed our suits and headed for the pool where I immediately faced a small problem—slippery, wet tile.

To be safe, I handed my crutches to Roix, plopped down on my butt, and painstakingly inched my way to the pool making every effort to appear graceful . . . uh-um.

It wasn't like this for the first part of my life. I was always in a rush, doing several things at once. A basket of laundry on one hip, a child balanced on the other, and maybe a couple of clothes pins clenched between my teeth, taking for granted my physical capabilities. What I have found since then is a profound sense of gratitude for motion. The effort that so many humans take for granted, the ability to walk from point A to point B, translates into sheer beauty for me.

When I finally reached the edge of the pool, that sunny afternoon in Costa Rica, I could see sunbathing hotel guests staring and wondering, *What the heck*? And when I dove in, all eyes were on me.

This always happens when I first appear in my one-piece bathing suit with the left leg sewn up. Sometimes, my audience will complement me on my vigorous swimming technique. Other times, they share a story about a family member or friend who, with an obvious disability, "would never dream of showing up in public wearing a swimming suit."

That day, I swam joyously, vigorously, lap after lap, feeling as if both my legs were kicking in unison, just as before. When I finished, I stood up at the end of the pool, balanced myself on one leg, shook my tail and said to the onlookers, "I bet you thought I was a mermaid!"

Because I'm active and physical and not embarrassed by my age or ashamed by my visible amputation, I like to believe that people think of me as inspiration rather than an object of pity. I thank God I'm able to stir positive rather than negative feelings—not only in my mirror but to others—that I am a woman still.

Cynthia

Cynthia solves the problem of fearing aging by not looking in the mirror.

———

Recently, I was lured into a facial demonstration in posh Jackson Hole, Wyoming, where a handsome, debonair, European stylist shoved an 110x magnifying mirror four inches from my face in the most glaring light ever invented and had the nerve to then ask me, "Show me what parts of this you would like to change." He almost convinced me to spend $10,000 on his fabulous treatments, now $4000, no wait, $2000. Oh for you, special lady, a one-time secret offer—but you must promise to zip your lips—all this for only $1500. But you must promise me, tell no one. Truly, I surprised myself by being almost in tears, not because I couldn't afford to spend $1500 on my face but because I looked so God-awful old.

That day I felt like shit about being old. And I felt helpless about it too. Now, a few days later, I solve the problem by not looking in the mirror. Fantasy does wonders.

So what's bad about being a woman of certain years: baggy, faded, spotty, dry skin, lost muscles, puffy eyes, squinty eyes, wrinkles, shortened waistline, widened waistline, lines where my calves used to be, flags waving when I raise my arms, neck that gets caught in my jacket zipper—to name a few.

How do I see myself? Well, I always felt beautiful as a teenager, young woman, mother, middle-aged woman. Now, at seventy, not so much. In fact, not at all. I recall an older woman walking down the dock when I was working on yachts (she was too) and me thinking how oddly wrinkled she looked. Now, I look that way. It's weird. I don't feel wrinkled at all, as long as I'm not seeing my reflection. I had tons of spirit before sixty-five—jazzy clothes, wild earrings, interesting shoes. I even wore fake eyelashes and long nails at one stage. Now, even wedge shoes feel unlike me. That makes me sad actually. I loved shoes as a businessperson and always wore high heels with lots of style. (In fact, my boss told me to make vice president I'd have to start wearing lower more conservative shoes! Boy was I pissed! How did Erin Brockovich get away with it???)

So, as I was saying, I don't feel beautiful now. From far away, fine, and I get compliments on how "young you look." But I figure they aren't looking very closely. Luckily, I have a great smile and I love smiling, so I think that's what saves me. I used to love my long neck but of course now it gets caught in a zipper. Gotta live with it. It's all I've got. And I'm a hell of a lot prettier than some people. I'm sure of that.

I use a few creams—but hardly ever really take care of my skin . . . no facials, go to sleep without *washing my face, rarely wear much makeup, don't eat right and barely exercise. It's lucky I look good at all. Never get pressure to have plastic surgery, because I don't hang out with those kinds of people. I'm full time camping now. No ironing boards, no closet of shoes, no chests of jewelry and certainly no fake eyelashes. Think of me sitting around a fire in the dirt. Plastic surgery would be so out of place. Not that I wouldn't love to have my jowls and neck raised, but who wouldn't at this age? I just figure I have to put up with it—so I chose to ignore it. My beauty is in my smile and my spirit, my enthusiasm for life. I'm very content with that—as long as you keep a mirror away!*

Melinda

Melinda discovered that when you change the way you see things, the things you are looking at change.

———

On a glistening, October day in San Diego, I walked the trail along the tranquil, blue bay, thinking about my imminent sixtieth birthday. A young girl in shorts and a tank top appeared on roller blades, her blond hair blowing in the sea wind. Into each stride, she put her entire perfect body, as if leaning into Life

15

itself. Watching her, some ancient feeling rekindled. I had been that girl once. I had leaned into life; now I leaned away. That is when a wave of unnamable emotion came over me. I can only say the feeling was one of not belonging, of being removed. Though I walked briskly, I felt as though I were moving in slow motion, disconnected from everything around me.

Friends kept asking, "How do you feel about turning sixty?" My glib response was: 'I'm okay with it. We're like fine wine. We keep getting better, right?' Sixty was just a number, and it had not bothered me much until that day. The unnamable feeling, I realized, was one of being suddenly old.

I hurried home, the blazing sun beating down on agitated water, seagulls squawking, the sea wind burning my face.

When I walked in the front door, my husband greeted me beaming, "Guess what? I just made a reservation for your birthday dinner at George's in LaJolla."

"Oh, great," I said, wishing I'd felt more enthusiasm.

Richard looked puzzled. "Would you rather go somewhere else?"

"No, no. I'm really happy about it." I forced a smile. "Thanks, Babe."

But I wasn't happy. I didn't have the feeling I had on other birthdays, when I'd be uplifted and thinking about all the reasons to celebrate. Yes, I was grateful, but I still struggled with yearning to be young again. Those times were gone, though, and I had to remind myself how blessed we've been. Having spent over forty years together, Richard and I created a litany of memories—being teenagers in love in Southern California, marrying, living in the Bay Area with our two daughters, then spending twenty years on a ranch in Southern Oregon, a condo on Maui, and now living near the beach in sublime San Diego.

The day of my birthday, I began dressing in my favorite, blue silk blouse and the turquoise necklace Richard had given me. But when I stood in front of the mirror in lacy underwear, I couldn't help but notice each pad of fat on my belly, my waist—everywhere. And I thought of the rollerblader's perfect body. What had happened to mine—the body that felt comfortable, even proud, in a swimsuit? I'd worked to stay slim, fit and healthy—exercising every day, doing yoga, always watching what I ate. Still, my body had betrayed me.

In my magnifying mirror, applying cover up, I noticed fine lines, dark spots and the beginning of a turkey neck. When I put on lipstick, I saw lines above my lips. Why hadn't I noticed these imperfections before? It was the rollerblader. It was all her fault.

That night, Richard and I sat on the deck at George's watching the glowing, orange sunset that reflected on the ocean below. We toasted with French wine and ate sumptuous food.

He held up his glass. "To the most beautiful woman in the world."

"Me?" I joked.

"Of course," he said, clicking his glass to mine. "Who else?"

"Well, I'm not going to argue, but I don't feel it."

"You may not feel it, but I see it."

If he saw me that way, I thought, why couldn't I? Hadn't I read about how we create our own reality? There was even a scientific principle. When you change the way you see things, the things you are looking at change. Somehow, this practice of changing the way I saw things didn't mesh with my life now. Aging was a hurdle I couldn't conquer. Now that I'm over seventy, when people ask how I feel about my age, I tell them, "Not a problem."

While walking on the bay recently, I saw another young rollerblader and my thought was: Yes, I'd been that girl once. But I've been softened by the chisel of experiences that carve sharp lines and sometimes break me open, so I can let in the real treasures.

Now, I'm looking at all the amazing, miraculous, magical gifts I've been given and with each stride, with my less-than-perfect but still strong body, I am leaning gratefully into this beautiful life.

J.J.

*"We can't reverse aging so we should
live with dignity."*

———

*There is nothing that is really bad about being
a Woman of a Certain Age. I miss my youthful body.
(LOL!) I have to keep this one covered with turtlenecks
and long sleeves. The days of bikinis and sexy stuff are
over. I like being here now. I might as well enjoy my
age; I can't reverse it so I choose to live with dignity.
I am grateful that I now know that I am a Spiritual
Being having a Human Experience.*

*As far as physical beauty is concerned, I knew
it was not a natural asset for me. I endeavor to be
attractive in actions and attitude and have since
learned that beauty is within and radiates the source
as light. Knowing I am divine has helped me to feel
beautiful from within.*

*Plastic surgery? No. Why should I? I keep my
efforts to manage my physical updates private. If I
chose to pursue that it would only be because it is my
choice, for me.*

L.A.

L.A. "Applauds nips and tucks? "Hell yeah!"

———

When Lenor asked me to write a piece in her new book about women and aging, knowing how I've spent a lifetime keeping that wolf away from my door, this song flashes into my head . . . War . . . what is it good for . . . Huh . . . sung by Edwin Starr back in 1969. Come on Girls, I know you all remember it! Only I substituted the word aging for war. Same thing, right? Here goes . . .

Aging, what is it good for "Huh-Yeah," Absolutely Nothin' . . . Say it again y'all. Listen to me . . . It ain't nothing but a Heart breaker . . . Friend only to the undertaker. . . . (Google it, it's a hoot!)

Now seriously, I have always enjoyed a life of looking and feeling young. To this day, I can shave fifteen-twenty years off my chronological age. I often get a doubting look when I say "Senior-please" at the movie theater.

I will let you in on some of my secrets. I have kept my face out of the sun. I have used a good sunscreen on the rest of my body. Most of my adult life I have belonged to a gym (and used it). I've always believed in a good diet. I take a hand-full of supplements morning and evening. I use good science-based skin creams. Nips and tucks? Hell yeah! I chose jobs that allow me to avoid alarm clocks and traffic. I think positive and avoid stress.

Susan

Susan knows that beauty is always in the eye of the beholder.

———

Do I think I'm beautiful at this age? Let's just say that I don't feel unattractive but no, I'm not beautiful in a glossy, perfect skin and idealized figure kind of way. Who is? But yes, I believe in my own beauty. It's not so much outward, but it's there, I'm sure of that.

I don't actually have a beauty regimen except to wash my face, drink lots of water and walk daily.

I used to wear makeup and loved it, but now that I'm older, I can't seem to find anything that doesn't irritate my skin and eyes within a couple of hours. Now days, I only wear makeup for special occasions, and only just a little.

A physician told me to wear a hat with at least a five-inch brim to give good sun protection. Despite that advice, most of the time you'll find me wearing a baseball cap with my pony-tail sticking out the back.

That seems to be my go-to style most of the time. Jeans and tees—I'm all about practical comfort.

I don't seem to have much vanity left but I do try to look nice most of the time. Really though, if beauty is in the eye of the beholder, anyone I come across has probably already made up their mind about what they see when they behold me. And what they see is all about them, not me. There will always be people that see older women as unappealing. Likewise, there will always be people who see beyond the outer trappings. Those are the only people I want to hang out with anyway.

Sharon C.

Sharon C. says yes to plastic surgery.

———

Plastic surgery is something I do believe in. Why not take advantage of modern science? I did have a face lift in my '50s and enjoyed looking younger for about ten years or so. Now, however, I have no interest and would just like to lose a few pounds but I must admit I don't do the work to accomplish this goal. I do eat healthy and exercise, but I enjoy my wine in the evening. It's all about making choices and I usually choose the wine!

Diana C.

Diana C. says she swims everywhere, figure and age notwithstanding.

———

When I was sixty-two years old, I decided to go to graduate school at the University of Oregon and get my PhD. Being an avid swimmer, I had thought I would take advantage of the opportunity to take swimming classes while I was there, but for two years I was so intimidated by the thought of appearing in a bathing suit in my mid-sixties in front of twenty-year-olds that I shunned swimming class. Finally, I told myself that that was ridiculous. If I wanted to swim, I should swim.

But if I were going to swim, I would need a swimsuit, since swimming in the nude is fine when I'm alone in the wilderness but not so appropriate in a college class. Just before the first term of my third year in graduate school, I swallowed my pride and marched into the swimming supply store close to campus to buy a swimsuit.

I was glad to see no other customers in the store. Skulking around the young salesgirl (probably a UO student and maybe even someone I would see in swimming class, I thought in panic) and then hiding behind the clothing racks, I looked for something appropriate. When I found a bathing suit I thought would do, I took it to the dressing room and wiggled into it. Then I took a deep breath and stepped in front of the mirror.

I was horrified. I looked like every middle-age woman who ever poured herself into a bathing suit— the bulky figure, the rolls of fat. There was no way I was going to appear in a college swimming class looking like this. I flung off the swimsuit, dropped it on the bench, and fled the store.

It took me another year before the desire to swim would overcome the embarrassment of my figure and my age, but before fall term the next year, I bought a swimsuit in a department store in town, where other women my age and my look might be buying swimsuits. When I got to campus, I signed up for swimming.

I tried to look nonchalant as I entered the women's locker room the first day of class, but that part wasn't too bad. I could dress in a private cubicle, and students were dressing and undressing hurriedly, having to get to class, so no one was paying attention to anyone else. But then I had to walk through the door into the pool room, and then I had to walk in front of the cluster of students on the bleachers to find a seat. The students were all, of course, decades younger than I, and, of course, they were eyeing each other, those young men and young women. I felt completely out of place and conspicuous, but I WANTED TO SWIM, so I stubbornly reminded myself that I had every right to be there and that I was there to swim, not to socialize or impress anyone. It's the swimming that's important, I said to myself, tucking my hair inside my swim cap and slipping into the pool with the other students.

Swim class was, in the end, one of the best things I did in graduate school. My instructor, Dan, the erstwhile coach of UO's erstwhile swim team, enjoyed having me in class—because I was an unusual student and because we were, after all, the same age. After I gave him a copy of my book, with the essay about swimming in Crater Lake, he liked to tease me about swimming in cold lakes. Most of the students ignored me, but to my surprise one or two every term were as friendly to me as to anyone else. They ignored my age and related to me as a fellow swimmer. It didn't take long before I was comfortable in class, bathing suit notwithstanding. I wasn't the worst swimmer, though I always swam in the slow lane. Many of the students had been on swim teams in high school. They didn't give me the time of day, but I didn't care. We were all there to swim and to learn something about swimming, both those who snubbed me and those who were friendly. I took swimming every term until I graduated and then all during the following year, *when I had a post-doc for teaching at UO. I loved swim class, irregardless of figure and age.*

Sharon B.

Sharon B. tells us what she sees reflected in the mirror.

———

OK, so I look in the mirror at times and wonder who's that round, white-haired person staring back at me and I realize it's me! In all my glory—tits sagging, ass drooping and crow's feet. I've never succumbed to Botox—not that I'm opposed to it but as an actress I need my frown lines still. It is what it is and thank God I have a husband who thinks I'm gorgeous. It's all in the eye of the beholder

As women of a certain age, what we want to see in the mirror is a reflection of our best selves. Whether we choose to accept our changing appearance or opt for a few nips and tucks is ultimately about getting comfortable in our bodies and feeling good about ourselves, whatever direction that takes.

Throw on that bathing suit and get in the water whatever your age or appearance! If you are smiling and enjoying yourself, how beautiful you become! Would you deprive yourself of the joy of swimming because you don't look like a movie star in your suit?

We learn that the only person who can make us feel less-than-beautiful is the person looking in the mirror.

Chapter Three

Rich in Love

Roix walks for me, I hear for him.

I am a woman of a certain age who is passionately in love with her husband after twenty-nine years of marriage. And I know I'm exceptionally lucky in this regard.

For me, the richness unfolds as an appreciation of my partner, and savoring each moment that we are together. It can be as simple as lying beside Roix at night, looking at him and smiling because he's sleeping peacefully and he's mine. Not to disturb him, I lightly touch his warm body. I'll be patient, as I'll experience the richness of his being, once morning comes, and he's awake and we can enjoy our coffee, read the newspapers and talk of our plans for the day, the next day or the next year.

We keep our love alive, in large part, because we support each other's interests. Sharing Roix's love of flying not only became a new and fascinating learning experience but also enriched my life and helped cement the depth of our relationship and commitment to each other, over the years, as in the following story:

A streak of blue appears, a filmy opening just broad enough for take-off. Our small plane shakes and vibrates as Roix revs up the engine. We are one with the plane as we race down the runway at eighty miles per hour. Our spirits lift as the plane climbs at a thousand feet per minute into the sky.

We're traveling to Los Angeles where I'm to be fitted with a computerized hydraulic leg. All the years I've been an amputee, it's been my dream to walk on a more refined leg. My prosthetist tells me this new leg will transform my life. I prayed he's right.

Forty-five minutes into our flight, the 14,179-foot volcanic cone of Mount Shasta rises just off to the left. She is my personal guardian, my beacon from afar. I pray to her for safe journeys and she never fails us, even when flying through high winds, ice storms and heavy rain.

Farther south, we can see the patch-quilt, farming communities of the San Joaquin Valley and I can see Tracy, the town where I lived the American dream, until my life suddenly and irrevocably changed forever.

I was riding my quarter horse, Champion, in a dusty, makeshift arena competing in a barrel racing event at Tracy's annual rodeo. Fans sat on worn fence posts as Willie Nelson blared from speakers. Champion stomped, snorted, and quaked as he burst through the paddock and ripped across the dirt towards the nearest barrel. We cut a tight turn and then he stretched his legs toward the second barrel and we achieved a perfect go around.

At high speed, Champion blasted toward the final barrel. He took the leap, lost his footing in the soft dirt and I floated, as if in slow motion, toward the ground. Champion hit with a thud atop my left leg. The saddle horn lodged in the space between my left leg and hip. Two years later, I found a hard lump in the exact area. It was cancer.

Continuing to fly south, I can see the vast wasteland of the Mojave Desert, and I am reminded of my own inner landscape, during that grievous time after the cancer diagnosis, when I often felt as desolate as the windswept land below us.

I would be happy to gaze out of the cockpit window all day, but the hours spent in the air begin to wear on my body. From the waist down I'm strapped into a bucket-like device that's attached to my prosthetic limb. The pressure around my hips and back intensifies. Roix only has to look at my face to know that I'm getting tired.

He calls in to Whitman Field, in the Los Angeles Basin, letting them know our position and intention to land. We receive no response. Roix calls again, "Copy?"

No response.

"We're too far out, Lenor. Take the controls, hold your position and fly the plane in wide circles."

"Okayyyy," I say, as I nervously clutch the yoke, thinking, *My God, he trusts me.*

We can hear the tower and other airplanes but they can't hear us. Roix grabs for the hand-held radio and continues to try and contact the tower.

"Keep an eye out for other planes," Roix says, scanning the sky as he punches in the frequency to Whitman Field.

I'm flying in controlled circles around Tejon Pass near Gorman. It's a little turbulent. Roix tells me to trim the nose up to slow down the plane.

"I can't get a response," Roix says. "We'll divert to Santa Paula airport. It's non-towered, so I'll be able to communicate with the hand-held radio."

Roix takes over the controls and I relax in my seat. As he brings us to a safe landing, I'm overwhelmed, not by fear, but by gratitude. I am in complete awe of this man—this strong, capable, rock of a man, who takes my life in his hands and always sees me safely home. Oh, the richness of love.

Tight quarters and one door on the passenger's side makes exiting the cockpit a close dance. Roix unbuckles his seat belt and gently slides over me. His aftershave lingers and I inhale deeply. He steps out and walks down the wing of the plane. From the back seat he grabs a blanket and spreads it out on the wing.

"Red carpet service, Madame?"

"Thank you, sir." I smile, slide my butt out on the wing, lift my fake leg straight up in a faux ballet stance, turn, and slide down on my personal "red carpet."

Roix ties down the plane and phones for a taxi. When it arrives, the driver asks if he can help unload the plane.

"Thanks. Get what's in the back seat, and I'll take care of the baggage compartment," Roix says.

The young man climbs up the low wing and peers into the back seat where my spare leg sits. He turns, eyes wide, and stares at Roix.

"It's okay, it's just my lady's leg. Stuff it in the trunk."

After recalling this story from the past, I return my attention to my morning coffee with Roix.

"Okay, my dear, what's on your agenda today?" I ask.

"Maybe I'll work on your trike."

Recently, Roix, bought a three-wheeled, electric tricycle that goes up to eighteen miles an hour, enabling me to ride alongside him, my friends, my children and grandchildren. Roix always thinks outside the box to work around my disability and make the impossible possible. It touches my heart when my girlfriends say, "We want a Roix, but we're happy you got him."

Sharon B.

Sharon B. reminds us that it really pays to find that person you can trust in any situation!

———

I love my husband He was my rock and he helped me through every minute of my cancers! His patience is beyond my realm, because I could never be as calm as he is; even during the roughest moments he was my strong, kind, compassionate man. It really pays to find that person you can trust in any situation!

My advice to anyone looking for the Prince Charming that you've read about in books. They probably don't really exist, however, that kind, reliable, soulful man you may have turned down at first glance, look closer and harder, because you may have passed by your Prince Charming.

Cathy

Cathy is glad she took a chance on internet dating.

———

I'm so happy I took a chance to find love on the internet. Let me tell you what happened. A friend of mine invited me on his yacht to go to Alaska. I've never been to Alaska. I thought it would be really fun. I had a great nine days enjoying his company; I learned to fish for shrimp and enjoyed the other couple that came with us.

I came home and a couple of weeks later I invited him to come and see where I lived. He said he didn't have time.

A month went by and I began thinking about the

wonderful time in Alaska and how I had enjoyed his company and the other couple as well. I think it was satisfying partly because I wasn't the third wheel on that trip. Being the third or fifth wheel had been something I had been experiencing, and it just gets old.

I decided then and there that I would really like to have a companion but where am I going to find one? Bars, no! Church? Probably not! Through friends? Probably not! So, this is where I took a chance. I did what many women of a certain age and living alone do NOT do—dating from the internet!

I decided to go on a dating site. I have talked to women that wouldn't take a chance because they were afraid of internet dating. "Too many crooks and kooks! I rather be alone."

Well, I took a chance and now I can honestly say that I'm happy and have met a love I hope to have for the rest of my life! Harry Kramer is eighty-seven years old, but you'd never guess. "Aging is a privilege," Harry said to me when we first met, and we're still going strong because we both believe it.

Diane

"Unfortunately, my husband's happy-go-lucky attitude did not last."

———

At the age of fifty, after fourteen years on my own, I met the love of my life. His name was Gordon Harris. He was handsome, a hilarious storyteller and was adored by everyone who met him. We were married for thirty wonderful years. During that time, our ranch bustled with activity. Although our children were grown when we married, our ranch became a gathering place where we hosted many weddings and parties. Friends and family from all over came to enjoy our rustic ranch celebrations. There were horses to ride on the fabulous trails. We had peacocks, chickens, dogs, cats, goats (as well as many wild critters), that kept the ranch full of life! At the age of seventy-three my husband started taking guitar and banjo lessons and learned to play and sing all kinds of country songs with his deep, resonant, Kentucky voice. Whenever we went out dancing, he would take the microphone and sing to everyone's delight! Unfortunately, Gordon's happy-go-lucky attitude did not last. I write of that sorrowful time later in this book.

J.J.

J.J. values her alone time.

———

Of course, I like romance but at this stage of my life I see no reason to be married. I'm not even sure a "live in" situation is something I want. While I am enjoying a nice relationship with a very kind man at present, living together is not something he wants either. And although we seem to be spending more and more time together, I really like my alone time too.

Susan

"It's a real joy to call my time my own these days."

———

I've been married a lot, to some good men mind you, but I can't seem to keep love alive. It appears that I'm more of a serial monogamist. I've made peace with it, but yeah, I've been married enough. I'm not going down that road again. I have had more than my share of romance, believe me, and there are things about having a committed partner that I'll miss, but I think this is my time for something completely different.

I'm alone now and . . . here it comes . . . I think I prefer it for this next stage of my life. I am finding it less complicated and more peaceful to simply live alone, not to mention having the pure freedom to do exactly what I want to do, whenever I want to do it, without having to negotiate or compromise. I know that sounds selfish, but I've spent my entire life as a second banana in one relationship or another and it's a real joy to call my time my own these days.

That being said, I realize I'm clearly not qualified to pontificate on how to stay in love, so I'll just say this, my parents' marriage lasted sixty-three years and they were pretty much unhappy about it every damn day of their lives. This might just have something to do with the fact that I can't seem to weather the rough patches in a relationship.

Despite my own failures, I am deeply envious of friends who have been married to one person for years and years. From where I'm sitting, it looks to me like they have developed a deep respect and appreciation for one another, something far beyond romance. No matter what ups and downs these couples experience, they just seem to find their way back to that core of deep regard for their spouse.

Yes, I'm sometimes sad that I'll never experience a life-long partnership like that. But I have had, and still have, life-long friendships that are as deep and as committed as any marriage and I've been blessed with some truly great loves and some dynamite adventures. I'm certainly not sad about that.

Cynthia

"I don't want to be the strongest one in the marriage."

I'm in a thirty-year relationship with my fun-loving, adventurous husband. We met in 1990, moved in together in 1992, moved to the Caribbean in 1994, got married in 2004 (after proving we could live together and work together 24/7 within 100 feet of each other (on a boat!) with strangers along for the ride much of the time (it was a charter yacht).

We did that for twenty years and now live full time in a 17' travel trailer. Traveling is what keeps us alive. Meeting new people and showcasing our lives to them reminds both of us on an almost daily basis how lucky we are and what fun we are having together.

If I could change anything, it would be to have my husband take care of me a little more than he does. I don't want to be the strongest one in the marriage, the one who figures things out and takes charge. But that's kind of the way I'm built (from my dad no *doubt) and luckily my husband is a happy-go-lucky, hunk of joy that keeps me laughing and exploring continually. So, what can I say?*

Shelly

"We do not replace people."

———

Most, if not all, relationships eventually end. Either one person leaves, or eventually someone dies. We all end up alone; I guess.

Since my husband passed away, I have to go on, but as a different person. I have a boyfriend now and he is a great and good man, but it isn't the same. We do not replace people.

I loved just being with my husband. Not 24/7 but you know what I mean. We could talk about everything and we always had each other's backs. We were always supportive of one another's happiness. He was my rock and I was his. We were "home" to one another.

Us, taking care of each other and our cats and dogs and our home, sharing laughter and sorrow was the best part of my life. I look at couples my age and think they are so lucky. I regret that I didn't really know how lucky I was until I lost my beloved.

Diana

Diana celebrates her late love and marriage.

———

I always thought I would get married. That's what girls did when they grew up. But when I grew up (?), I became a hippy, and hippies were philosophically against marriage. I did have my as-though-married relationship, which, not unusual in a marriage, fell apart, after five years.

Facing life as a single woman, I thought, I'll be dadgum if I live my life with a hole in it for some man to fill up. So I lived a full, rich, happy life as a single woman, though I always assumed I would get married.

Then I hit menopause. The assumption faltered.

But life is full of surprises.

In 2014, when I was seventy, I met Mike Kohn when both of us joined the board of the Applegate Trails Association. We soon discovered great pleasure in each other's company: skiing, reading, sharing good food and wine, and, above all, hiking—on Corsica, in Italy, on many trails in the Applegate, the Siskiyou Mountains, the Cascades.

After five years, we decided it was time to walk down the aisle together, too.

Suddenly I was thinking about wedding dresses, wedding flowers, wedding dinner. Planning took months of detailed organization, much of it done with me by Mike's side while he underwent chemotherapy. He had been diagnosed with esophageal cancer shortly after I met him. Treatment was successful then, but now, four years later, the cancer had returned.

We were so giddy with wedding excitement (to the amusement of nurses and medical personnel) even cancer couldn't dampen our enthusiasm.

Mike finished chemo two weeks before the wedding.

On the wedding day, our guests and all the wedding party except me, my brother, Lee, and my grandnephew Isaac assembled at River Crest Ranch on the Applegate River. My son, Ela, was playing music on his large sculpture-instruments. At a signal from him, Mike, radiant with excitement, led the equally jubilant wedding guests to a trail on the cliff above the river. Ela blew a conch. Everyone waited.

What they didn't know they were waiting for was the bride's entrance by canoe down the fast-flowing Applegate River.

The river had been so fast that spring that Mike and I had worried about a bridal entrance by canoe. The weekend before the wedding, a river-guide friend came to assess the river for us.

"No problem," he said, and took us on a successful

practice run.

The morning before the wedding rehearsal, Lee, a competent river runner, Isaac, a canoeing novice and enthusiastic bowman and I, passenger, made another practice run. We launched easily from our spot upriver and were hidden from the view of the wedding site. Lee faced the canoe upstream, then turned it into the current. Down we went. The tricky bit came at the end of the run, when we had to swing into an eddy to keep from being swept into the rapids. Unfortunately, Lee started the turn too late and had to fight the current to keep us from hitting the rapids. He managed to land us successfully, to everyone's relief.

A few hours later, when we came down the river for the rehearsal itself, Lee underestimated the turn, and we banged into the large rock at river's edge, bow head-on, BAM!

The day of the wedding, Lee, Isaac, and I waited in the canoe, upriver, me in my long, white, wedding gown, carrying a colorful, bridal bouquet. At the sound of the conch, Lee cried, "That's it!" Isaac cast off, and Lee turned us into the current.

As the wedding guests caught sight of us coming down the river in our red canoe, they gave a great cheer. I waved my bouquet high over my head. I was told later that though I was beaming, Isaac looked terrified as Lee made what turned out to be a very accurate turn into the eddy with perfect timing. To *the cheers of the crowd, we landed gracefully on the beach. Mike met me with a gigantic hug, then led me through the crowd to the wedding arch. The throngs followed.*

Many people told me later it was the best wedding they had ever attended. "It was so full of love," they said, as though the happiness emanating from Mike's and my love had ignited everyone's love. The entrance by canoe was everyone's favorite part, but people also mentioned the spiral (when my daughter-in-law led the whole company, linked by hands, in a spiral around Mike and me) and the proclamation of marriage that our officiant (Mike's good friend) had written for everyone to recite, line by line after him:

> *"It is our honor,*
> *here at the holy center of the universe,*
> *in this crucible of love and truth,*
> *with the blessing of our ancestors,*
> *of the rivers, mountains, and forests,*
> *and the support of all living beings,*
> *to pronounce Mike and Diana husband and wife."*

At the end of the evening, after the dinner and the dancing and the cake, as Mike and I passed through the crowd to our get-away car, our guests tossed lavender buds over us. The air was scented with lavender.

We spent our nuptial night at a B&B in town, riding high with excitement and joy. A wedding like that, we knew, could only happen for those as rich with love as Mike and I.

Crossing Borders

Marriage is a foreign country
which I'll enter in May.
I don't cross the border
as a refugee
fleeing loneliness and unhappiness
in my home country
or as an emigrant
leaving one country
in hopes of a better life
in the other.
I've got my passport
(the passport is love)
not a limited-stay visa
to see how I like things
but permanent residency
in the new country
promising joy.

Whether we have found the love of our life, or are navigating a difficult marriage, or even soldiering on alone, love remains a keystone in all of our lives. Women of a certain age know how to value love when it's there, support it to make it thrive, and move on with grace when it's absent. Whichever way we look at it, we can recognize real love for the rare treasure that it is and never take it for granted.

Chapter Four

Love of Travel

"Let us step into the night and pursue that flighty temptress, adventure."

~ J.K. Rowling

Why travel? Because it can become all too easy to settle into our comfortable routines. There's a lot to be said for the security of home and a set of habits that nurture us, but it's a slippery slope that can go from a healthy routine to a stifling rut.

Getting out of our comfort zone broadens our outlook and sharpens our senses. Whether you're sitting by a campfire, roaming the oceans on a yacht, or just going for a walk down a new street, the view is going to be decidedly different than from your living room.

Roix and I were in our early sixties when a two-week vacation to Costa Rica turned into twelve years of periodic traveling and living throughout Central America.

Looking back, I can't think of another man with whom I'd have ventured off to third world countries with so little foresight. I didn't even factor in our ages or our disabilities—Roix's lack of hearing and my loss of limb.

Costa Rica was life changing.

Our first night, we stayed in San Jose, the capital of Costa Rica. We checked into the Grand Hotel where the city's nightlife unfolded in front of our hotel's crowded, outdoor restaurant. Exhausted from our flights, we still didn't want to miss out on the exciting scene, so we ordered dinner and drinks and were thoroughly enchanted by the spirited marimba music and the beautiful young men and women promenading round the Plaza, flashing their dark eyes.

The next morning, Roix left the hotel looking to convert U.S dollars into *Colines*. He soon found out that dollars could be exchanged in alleyways, where gullible foreigners, unused to Latin-style haggling, sometimes suffered unfortunate losses. I marveled at how Roix, with his hearing impairment and no knowledge of the Spanish language, could bargain with these transient bankers and always come out ahead. There's something about his towering presence—like John Wayne before a quick draw—that gets things done.

After touring the city for a couple of days, we asked our hotel manager where we could go for a little side trip. "Parismina is where you must go," he said, "It's in the rain forest north of

Limon, on the Atlantic coast—only accessible by boat."

We were anxious to see as much of Costa Rica as possible, so we hopped on the hotel's mini-van and after three hours, the driver abruptly jerked to a stop in the jungle alongside a steep incline that descended into a muddy river.

"This is your drop off point," the driver announced. "Paco is waiting below on his boat. He'll take you through the canals to Parismina. Adios."

Confused, I looked at Roix. "Do we know exactly where we're going?"

"Parismina! Let's move it. We've got to get down this bluff and on to that . . ." he flinched, "boat down there, before it gets dark."

So, I shimmied my way down the rough bank using my artificial leg for leverage, while Roix walked ahead hauling our suitcases and loaded them onto the small, dilapidated, wooden boat.

It was hot and humid. Our little boat putt-putted down the river spewing smoke, nearly drowning out the sounds of the tropical birds in the overhanging trees, as we squirmed through pure jungle.

We continued downriver, marveling at the tropical rain forest and its myriad of birds. There were toucans with large, sharp, colorful beaks and macaws that flaunted their scarlet plumage as they sailed through the trees.

Along the river's edge, we caught glimpses of great white herons, with elongated legs and necks and harpoon-like beaks and giant bird's nests cast in the shape of tear drops hanging from trees. We spotted iguanas, some of them four or five feet long, lounging high up in tall trees where one might expect to see only birds. And, most curious, we caught sight of several small reptiles, called "Jesus Lizards," running across the water with great speed.

The sky grew dark and the river narrowed. I began to feel a little anxious as the encroaching jungle became nearly impassable.

"This is so mystical," Roix said in tones of wonder, utterly impervious to his spouse's unvoiced apprehensions. "It's absolutely amazing."

Just before dark, we beached the canoe along a sandy canal bank. After we gathered our things, Paco led us up to a row of one-room, palm-thatched cabinas perched high on stilts. After settling in, we joined Paco for dinner in a larger cabina used as a communal dining room for guests, however there were no other guests. After dinner, Paco invited Roix to go crocodile hunting.

"Yeah! I'd love to go. When?"

"Now," Paco, said.

"What?" I exclaimed. You're going to go crocodile hunting at night?"

"It's perfectly safe; *no problema*," Paco said calmly. "The crocs are only three to five feet long."

"But . . . but," I muttered . . .

"We go in a canoe," Paco continued.

When I opened my mouth to register even more alarm, Roix cut in. "Please, Lenor, I want to hear what he's got to say."

"We go slowly and quietly along the riverbanks, using only

flashlights to seek out the crocs. They're easy to spot at night because when we flash the light on them, their eyes turn a bright red-orange color. We don't hurt them. We just pick them up by the neck in a certain way and they go stiff. We take a photo and then release them."

And so it was to be.

That night, Roix finally touched, or I should say dangled, a crocodile in the tropical rainforest of Costa Rica.

A few days later, back in San Jose, we rented a car, bought a map of Costa Rica and headed for a village called Nosara on the Pacific Coast. Ostensibly, we were headed there to deliver a check to a builder who was working on an American friend's new house in the area. But in truth, we were ready for a new adventure.

Due to the dusty, bumpy dirt roads—or sometimes lack of roads—it took us far longer than we had expected to reach Nosara. It was nearly dark when we saw a sign leaning sideways: "Nos . . . 12 kilometers." We couldn't make out the rest of the letters because of the dirt on the sign, but assumed from our map that "Nos," must be the beginning letters of Nosara . . .

We drove on, not certain as to whether we were going in the right direction or not. The night grew darker. We hadn't passed another car in a long time and I began to feel uneasy.

Then we came upon the first of several rivers that had to be crossed to reach Nosara. The bridge didn't look secure, so Roix jumped out of the car, flashlight in hand, and inspected it.

"I don't think it's safe to cross," he said, as he shined the light under and over the bridge against the jungle backdrop.

"My God, Roix, what'll we do?"

"Cross it," he said, with not a glimmer of fear or apprehension. "But first, I've got to close up the car's grill opening so water won't seep into the engine when we cross. I think there's some cardboard in the trunk. Give me a minute."

Roix deftly slit the cardboard and covered the grill in the promised minute.

"Okay, honey, this ought a do it," he says, patting the hood of the car.

We traversed the river by the meager light of a quarter moon and the illumination of our car's headlights. Roix sought out eddies where he could see water ripping over gravel, knowing it would be shallow in that area of the river.

"We've got to keep this car moving without stopping, but not too fast. We'll plow through the water until we get to the other side."

Once we were safely up on the riverbank, I looked at Roix in relief. "We made it!" I gasped.

"Only five more rivers to cross," he winked. "Hopefully, they'll have bridges."

They did not.

Negotiating five more crossings of unknown jungle rivers in the dark of night, admittedly, was a white-knuckle experience, at least for me. Yet, I soon grew accustomed, even excited, whenever we braved another bridgeless river. It was all part of our adventure.

On and on we drove in search of the village of Nosara. There were no streetlights, just small dirt roads leading mysteriously into the jungle. At last, we saw a sign that read Taipei Hotel.

"Stop, Honey," I shouted, "there's a hotel!"

"Where?"

"I don't know, but it must be down that road . . ."

Around a bend we saw a brightly lit hotel, under a canopy of lush, green jungle.

Exhausted, we collected our bags and walked into a festive, outdoor, garden lobby with tile floors, high wood beam ceilings and a lively bar. We couldn't believe our luck—an oasis in the jungle offering a couple of cold beers and a room for the night.

The following day, Roix and I found the primitive village of Nosara, and Señor Jose, the builder.

"Shoe leather express?" Roix laughed, handing Jose the envelope with the check.

Perplexed by the English idiom, yet happily surprised and thankful for the service, Jose offered to show us around Nosara and the internationally famous surfing beaches nearby.

Within hours, Roix and I fell in love with Nosara and asked Jose if he knew of any properties for sale. He immediately drove us to a location in a National Reserve, overlooking the jungle and on the edge of the Pacific Ocean. It was a half-acre property with a twenty-year-old, crumbling foundation swamped with unruly foliage.

"It looks like the Mayan Ruins," said Roix in awe.

We bought it in on the spot for a song and a year later went back to Costa Rica hoping to begin construction on a small *Casita* which ultimately turned into a 2,800 square foot Villa. It was a bold move, especially in the middle of a jungle in a third world country.

We hired Jose, the same guy we bought the lot from, who was a well-known local builder. We assumed he was trustworthy.

It took time and effort. Roix had to fly back and forth several times a year to keep an eye on Jose and work alongside the laborers correcting their mistakes and making sure they didn't siesta on the job. The language barrier was torture and money transactions frustrating. Even more alarming, Jose would vanish when we were not there to move on to another American's project—using our money.

Finally, when Jose announced the villa was finished, we could hardly contain our excitement. Yet when we arrived, there were no windows or doors, no toilets, no sinks and no running water. We moved in anyway and invited our neighbors to a "house-warming," adding, "please bring a chair and, kindly, leave it."

After four arduous years, our planned small *Casita* had turned into a gorgeous villa with 24' *pachoti* wood ceilings, Italian tile floors, terraces with unobstructed views of the jungle reserve and ocean below. Like Frances Mayes' ordeal in *Under the Tuscan Sun*, "the time and effort, the agony and ecstasy were a labor of love."

Living as American expats in the tropics of Central America was an extraordinary adventure. Nosara became our second home for three to four months each year and every day presented us with a new challenge. Though we have since sold the villa, I would not trade the experience for anything.

Even as the years advance, I continue to wonder what's

around the next corner and wish to go explore. It's always about the journey, not the journey's end.

Cathy

Cathy traced the footsteps of Ernest Hemingway.

———

Last year, I shocked my family and friends when I decided to walk the El Camino also known as the Way of Saint James. My friend, Mary, and I traveled with National Geographic to Spain and walked ten to fifteen miles a day for nine days. The movie, The Way, with Martin Sheen, helped promote the popularity of the walk all over the world.

We traced the footsteps of Ernest Hemingway through Pamplona. Also, we explored spectacular cathedrals and monasteries and encountered Roman sites and mountain villages. We stayed in historic Paradors built centuries ago. We walked the foothills of the Pyrenees Mountains and high plains that stretch across much of Central Spain. Each morning, before the walk, as well as at night, I repaired my feet and toes, with medicine and Band-Aids from my first aid kit.

Blisters were a common problem. I thought what am I going to do? My feet are killing me but I was *determined to finish the walk and not ride in the van that was ready any time. My friend, Mary, and I were the oldest (74) in the group of fourteen and we finished!*

Diana

Diana describes her thrilling hike in the Dolomite mountains in Italy.

———

Dead tired and dizzy with exhilaration, Mike and I sloughed our packs at the Rifugio G. dal Piaz and clasped each other in an ecstatic hug. We had come to the end of the twelfth and final day of hiking the Alta Via 2, in Italy's Dolomite Mountains—98 miles, at altitudes between 6000 and 9800 feet, ascending in total 29,530 feet. Exultation trumped exhaustion. When we told the proprietor at Rifugio dal Piaz that we had just completed AV 2, he grinned and said did we want to see our rooms first or have a beer first?

Beer won, hands down. We clinked glasses, our faces beaming. The proprietor brought us each another beer, on the house. We beamed and beamed.

I was, as far as I can tell, the oldest person on the trail, during those two weeks in September 2016. Once, a woman we met on the trail asked Mike how old he was. When he said, "Sixty-six," she crowed, "I beat you. I'm sixty-eight." I couldn't help myself. I said, coyly, "I'm seventy-two." (She didn't hike the whole trail, either, as Mike and I did.)

The AV 2 was varied, beautiful, exciting, sometimes dangerous, always challenging. Most of it was in bare-rock Alpine terrain, but there were also long grassy walks. It was so steep in places that the villages below looked like child's toys dumped on a floor. "Sometimes steep, sometimes steeper, sometimes steepest," Mike said. A lot of the steepest, highest places on the trail were covered with gravel scree, as treacherous as ping-pong balls. One of the characteristic sounds of the Dolomites was the scrunch of a foot sliding down loose rock.

Sometimes, we had to climb practically vertical walls. Securing our hiking poles onto our packs, we started up, searching for footholds and handholds, hauling our bodies up by the iron cable, climbing up (or down) vertical ladders—hiking aids called via ferrata. More than once, I had to stretch my legs to take steps more suitable for longer legs than mine. Partway up, I would look down an enormous distance. Hikers on the trail below looked like cars seen from an airplane.

Often the crumbling trails traversing hillsides were so narrow the foot barely had a purchase. Holding onto the via ferrata prevented a possible tumble hundreds, if not thousands, of feet into the chasms below. "What do you do," I asked, "if a group of hikers is coming towards you in such an impassable place?"

"Kiss," came the reply.

Frequently we heard the distant music of cow or sheep bells. At one point, the trail took us through a herd of peacefully grazing cows (and an intimidatingly large bull), their bells clanging musically on all sides of us with every nod of a cow's head. Once, when we topped a pass, we were met not with the pastoral effect of cow bells but with the decidedly urban roar of race car engines. Far below us, in Passo Cereda, where we were headed, the San Martino International Rally was taking place. The rest of the day was haunted with the distant roar and obligatory backfiring of race cars, a strange sound to be flung into the Dolomites.

The danger was not inconsiderable—slipping and falling on the scree, twisting or breaking an ankle, missing a turn in the trail, hitting your pack against an overhanging rock as you leapt a chasm and getting knocked down the mountain, getting so tired you stumbled. At most points, a fall would send you over the cliff, but when Mike did actually tumble off the trail, on the longest descent of the entire Alta Via 2 (4000 feet in two miles), he was on what was probably the only grassy bank on the whole descent. He said that as he fell and rolled down the bank, he was so relieved not to be walking that he would have been happy just to keep on rolling.

On another day, as we were climbing up a rocky pass with some via ferrata and some free-climbing (when we wished for via ferrata!), I saw a small, white plaque on a rock with the names of two Italians, a date, and the words, nos amici. When Mike joined me at the top, I told him I was glad I didn't have to put up a plaque with his name on it.

Whenever I reached the top of a pass at last, with peaks all around me and the valley unbelievably distant, I was, each time, unbelievably ecstatic.

Walking the Alta Via 2 ranks as one of the great achievements of my life: from Plose to Rifugio dal Piaz, day after day, up mountains and down, six, seven, eight, nine hours a day, achieving passes (sometimes three in a day), making steep descents— the rock-climbing, the via ferrata, up steep chimneys, across vertical ways—the razor-edge walks—the dizzying heights—the marmots and the Alpine goats (chamois)—the flowers, purple and yellow—the rifugios in rock settings, where supplies had to be brought in by helicopter—the impossible passes— each place demanding its own memory but each memory isolated from the whole. At which rifugio? On which day? Up which pass? Which canyon, which magnificent view, which ferrata, which impossible climb, which impossible descent? Pictures, images, memories come in flashes. How can I convey the experience? No one would believe it, even if I could. That's because it was impossible—impossibly steep, impossible to climb that slope, impossible to work that hard and love every minute, a walk that made both Mike and me impossibly strong, impossibly fit, impossibly ecstatic.

Cynthia

"Travel is my life."

———

As a kid, I didn't travel much, and with my children, we traveled to camp and canoe the rivers of Missouri and to Florida for grandparents.

After a divorce, the kids and I traveled cross country in both directions, hiked down and up the Grand Canyon, went scuba diving in San Diego and even in Cozumel. They had the travel bug too.

When my kids were grown, they moved to the West Coast. I moved to San Diego and met Winston, the Sagittarius whose been traveling with me ever since. Travel is my life and has been since 1994 when we moved to the Caribbean to run a pirate bar. From there, becoming yacht captain and chef, we ran mega-yachts up and down the Caribbean, the Atlantic to New England, the Pacific to British Columbia and Mexico, and more. Almost non-stop. It was a fabulous lifestyle.

When we retired, we couldn't imagine life in a house . . . so we bought a travel trailer, named her "Yacht Enough" and have been criss-crossing the country ever since.

Susan

My mother once said that if you wait for someone else to join you, you might miss your chance to go.

———

A while back, I found myself with the money and time to take a trip to Ireland, someplace I always wanted to go. However, the timing was such that I had no one to go with me. I asked friends and family but no one was available just then. So, I figured, what the hell, just go alone. Some people thought I was nuts, but it was wonderful. I was completely free to pursue whatever I wanted; I could dawdle through museums, poke around in little shops, take long walks through the countryside, or sit in a pub and listen to music. I thoroughly enjoyed myself and I'm so glad I got to visit the country of my heritage. I made lots of friends *and had a whale of a time!*

My mother once said that if you wait for someone else to join you, you might miss your chance to go. So now, whenever I get the itch to go someplace, I'm as apt to go alone as not.

Is it as much fun to travel alone as it is with a partner, companion or a best friend? Truthfully, I suppose it depends on the company. I'm not intimidated in the least to venture out on my own, never have been. I know how to be careful and how to make friends—good skills to have no matter where you are.

When I was a corporate minion, I traveled for business a lot, in fact, weekly: airports, hotels, rental cars, hurry hurry. I got pretty burned out. I just wanted to go home and stay there. For a long time after that, staying home is what felt like a luxury.

Lately, I've been thinking of getting an RV and touring around the countryside for a few years. Imagine the thrill of visiting places that interest me?

There's a thought! Wildlife refuges, historical sites, and museums are typically a yawn for others, but now I can do that and not feel the least bit guilty! I can follow the entire Lewis and Clark trail if I feel like it. I can haunt every quilt shop in fifty states! In between I can stop in to see all the friends and relations that I love and hang out with them. That just sounds like fun.

Women of a certain age know that traveling to a new destination is as exhilarating as arriving. The road can offer so many opportunities for growth and insight if we're willing to open ourselves to new experiences. It doesn't have to be expensive, exotic or dangerous to find a different view that might re-awaken a sense of wonder in us. On any sunny day, Roix and I might load up our bicycles and peddle through the park or out to a local winery. Sometimes that's all I need to reignite my creative juices while getting exercise and whipping up a little joy.

Chapter Five

Balancing Act

"The great art of life is sensation, to feel this we exist, even in pain."

~ Lord Byron

Most women of a certain age seek ways to minimize the effects of challenges in order to maximize their enjoyment in life. It's an extremely rare bird that never experiences a physical trial of one kind or another—whether it's a sudden illness, chronic pain, or a lifelong condition.

Chronic pain is something most women of a certain age live with on a daily basis. I, too, tolerate chronic pain from the effects of my amputation. I suffer a discomfiture that is not ordinary and is mostly misunderstood. It's called phantom limb pain and I've been dealing with it for over forty-eight years.

The question I'm most frequently asked by family and friends—even strangers—is "What is phantom limb pain? And do you still have it?" Most people are amazed that it's still with me and has not faded over the years.

It won't be difficult to describe as it hit without warning just two nights ago, with an alarming blow that scrambled my body's rhythm. A direct, searing flash to my non-existent left ankle, arch and big toe targeted the most sensitive parts until, ultimately, the whole leg was under attack along with electrical sparks smacking me every three to five minutes.

I grabbed my bottle of Vicodin, knowing I can sometimes curb the pain, if I pop two pills within minutes of the first jolt. More often, however, fearing becoming addicted as I was during the first months after my surgery, I wait in hopes that the phantom devil will grow bored and retire on his own. Wishful thinking, though, because he never does.

So on this night, I did not take a Vicodin. I'll try not to give in. I'll talk the phantom down.

"Damn you!" I screamed when I was belted again.

"Fuck you!" I repeat with each assault, "Fuck you!"

It was as if we were punching it out in the ring. Me shouting explosive, malevolent words and the phantom thumping back even harder.

In between wallops, desperate, I jumped up and crutched to the kitchen, poured a shot of brandy, gulped it down and with the bottle dangling from my hand, hurried back to bed before he could take aim once again.

Too late! He punched even harder, leaving me stunned as I leaned against the doorway.

"Leave me alone, you bastard, leave me alone!" I used more vile words to fight the demon while I played this game with the drug.

The running conversation in my head was: "Take the pills. Don't. Have another drink. Don't."

I finally gave in. I set aside the brandy, but swallowed two Vicodin pain pills, applied ice and asked my husband to please massage the area of the amputation. Roix, lying next to me, did as asked, and I waited for relief.

Once in slumber, thankfully, the phantom sleeps too.

I awoke the next morning with no pain but with the familiar, galvanizing buzzing that most amputees experience around the clock.

As a young woman and up until now, I've tried to neither fear the phantom nor condemn him for his persistence. Yes, he will be back to take his random shots. This I know for sure. I've learned that two pain pills, ice, heat, massage and the comfort of Roix will be enough to make the phantom sleep . . . at least for a while.

Thankfully, it's not an everyday occurrence. I can go for weeks without an episode. When I feel the beginnings, a mere reflection of what is to come, I immediately embrace the spasm by holding and kneading the area. I try to evoke feelings of love, as I try to calm it down. I do this because it's my body and I don't want all the fuss to work into another phantom tantrum.

Even when younger, and now in my '70s, I've tried to interpret the phantom as a sensation rather than pain. This sets me up for a far better experience. And by not thinking of it as a curse, but rather a blessing—God's way of leaving an imprint powerful enough to hint to the missing leg that it's lying right alongside its partner as before. For me, this works as a positive rather than a negative sentiment, soothing the leg's hurt feelings that it's not here anymore. By re-framing my reaction to this pain, I alter my perception to make my condition more bearable.

Sharon B.

"Get the cancer out and save my life."

———

I just turned seventy in 2020 and my body has certainly had a few kinks along the way—a hip replacement and thyroid cancer, but to me, they made me appreciate the body I've been given.

Here was my little glitch. I went to have my throat checked out with my speech pathologist. She looked at me funny when she had her hands on my throat and said, "I don't remember feeling this lump."

Ok, I feel it, so what now? Off to a specialist at UCSF. He looked at me and said, "I think it's a goiter, but you are an actress and we should just remove the lump." So that sounded like a fair and balanced review of my situation. A biopsy was done then and there. About forty-five minutes went by and then in walked the doctor with a strange look on his face and said, "Its cancer."

What the fuck! You just said I had a goiter. Now you are saying the C-word? I teared up instantly not because my mortality was at risk but because my husband was in the room and he had lost his first wife to cancer. I thought this could not be happening to him again. So, the doctor proceeded to tell me, "Sharon you'll die by getting hit by a bus before you'll die from thyroid cancer." Oh well, I guess that was the good news.

So, three weeks later, after singing my heart out as Lumiere in Beauty and the Beast, I went in to get my throat slit open. Mind you, as a singer and actress that alone was a daunting thought and as the doctor was wheeling me down the hall he said, "I cannot guarantee that I won't hit your vocal cord." Well, that's encouraging. I just looked up at him and said, "Get the cancer out and save my life."

I woke up after the surgery and the first thing I said to my husband was, "I lived." That's when he realized the doctor did not hit my vocal cord much to my husband's dismay—ha—ha.

After two years, my singing voice never returned to its fullest but I just take one, small, thyroid *medication and have not had another incident again. I'm proactive about seeing my endocrinologist, taking my meds and just having a great attitude which I believe is the real key to surviving anything that comes along in your life that might throw you for a loop. I try to make healthy choices with occasional treats. After all, what's life without ice cream?*

Then, after all of that, I was lucky to have been diagnosed with breast cancer ! Why lucky?

Well, it was a non-aggressive, slow-growing cancer, not even considered a stage one! But here's the really lucky part; I was given a reduction and lift at the same time they got all my cancer out. All-inclusive treatment and you should see my new boobs!! Wowza! They are perky and so nice looking that even I look down and say, "Whose boobs are those?"

I am a very lucky lady, thyroid cancer two years ago and now this but I am a warrior-women grateful for every minute!

Susan

"Finding balance and being healthy is about making lifestyle changes.

———

I have lupus. It sucks. It eats up far too much

of my energy. I baby myself when it's called for and push myself when I need to. I visit the doctor when I have to.

When I was first diagnosed, I was all about doing what the doctor said to do. I took the pills, went to physical therapy and ta-da! . . . the steroids caused me to gain a TON of weight and wrecked my stomach and ruined my teeth. A few years later, I decided to get off all the meds, lose the weight, and do everything as naturally as possible: eat healthy, take a small handful of supplements and voila I'm no worse, and actually better in some ways.

I've learned that finding balance and being healthy is about making lifestyle changes like getting the stress out of your life, getting enough sleep, doing some kind of regular moderate exercise and eating your vegetables. You know, all the stuff our mothers and grandmothers have been telling us to do for centuries. I've also been doing yoga for years and it's the single most effective thing I've found to deal with chronic pain.

Bottom line is, I don't like to talk about my health. I don't enjoy being around people who talk a lot about theirs either.

My plan is to be as healthy and happy as possible for as long as possible and then just die. No lingering. No complaining. Wish me luck.

Diana

"What do we mean when we talk about balancing our daily life with a spiritual self . . . ?"

———

I've been having kind of a rough time lately, dealing with my sister's death, from Lewy body dementia, then immediately afterwards completely blowing my chances to get a job I wanted by doing badly at the interview, then spinning into despondency for having done that. On top of that, it's fall term, and I miss teaching, since I was forced into retirement last spring.

Last weekend my soon-to-be-fiancé, Mike, and I hiked into the Red Buttes Wilderness Area. Partly, I wanted to make sure I could still do a difficult hike, after a summer of inactivity (knee injury, excessive heat, wildfire smoke), and partly, of course, to see what the trail would offer.

Had I forgotten that every trail offers wonders? Had I forgotten that the mountains are a sure antidote for what ails me?

After the first, steep mile, we entered an enchanted forest, where a thin, white line of snow turned every-thing it touched into lace—every needle of every pine tree, every stone, root, or limb, every branch of every bush, every scabrous edge of bark. Gradually the snow deepened, until we were kicking through a half inch or more. Where the sun had visited, briefly, before it tucked behind the mountain again, winter-brown stalks rose from wet earth. We walked from snow-sprinkled woods to sun-melted patches of browns to shaded open spaces where bushes, earth, rocks, and sticks were painted white.

Flourishes of ice decorated the edges of Frog Pond. At Cameron Meadow, just under the Mt. Emily ridge, ice had spell-bound the pool into silent immobility. On the Cameron Meadows trail, autumn leaves covered the ground like a fabric of yellow and brown hues: tawny, flaxen, buff, terra cotta, tortoiseshell.

Once, when I stopped to take in the beauty of the forest—that carpet of yellow, the early afternoon dusk, the stark linearity of a clump of tall, white-skinned, madrone trunks, I saw a bear clambering down one of those long, slim, madrones, after a meal of berries at its top, descending hind end first, looking now over the right shoulder, now over the left, scooting as fast as a fireman down a pole—a rolling black ball on a white trunk.

The next day, I had a conversation with a friend about what we mean when we talk about balancing our daily life with a spiritual self (religion aside). I'm not sure I know. I long ago gave up the struggle about whether or not I am developing my spiritual

*self. It doesn't seem to matter. What does matter
and is probably relevant to that spiritual self I claim
not to understand or to nourish is that being on the
mountain trail with its white beauty, its fallen leaves,
and its galloping bear has left me a better person
today than I was before.*

Picking Cherries

Yesterday, climbing the cherry tree
to harvest the rich red globes,
I thought about my eighty-year-old father
saying, when my nineteen-year-old son
offered to clean gutters for him,
"Better let me do it.
It's dangerous on the roof."

I thought of that when
the ladder I was climbing
into the cherry tree
slipped and teetered
and I hurriedly stepped
into the crotch of the tree,
leaving the ladder gently swinging.

If my son were here and said,
"Let me pick those cherries for you,"

I would say, yes, thank you.
But I enjoy climbing high into the tree
where the best and the most cherries dangle.
I enjoy pulling branches
towards me with my pruning hook,
holding them doubled back with one hand,
plucking their cherries with the other,
stretching to reach the swinging fruit
that I drop into the bag slung over my wrist.

I thought of the dangers:
reaching too far
breaking the limb I was holding
stretching beyond the balance point.
I thought: *I should have brought my cell phone.*
I thought: *Should a seventy-year-old woman be*
climbing trees?
But mostly I thought: *cherry pie, cherry preserves,*
cherry tarts, cherry ice cream.
I thought how beautiful the dark red clusters were,
how lovely the breeze through the tree,
how charming the birdsong from the woods,
how much I enjoy
still being able
to climb a tree
and pick its cherries.

Every woman of a certain age navigates physical challenges of some kind or another. I experienced mine at a young age and I've lived with it for many years. By accepting my loss, and not exhibiting to others that I am in pain, or that I'm embarrassed by my circumstance, I'm able to smile brightly even when I'm, let's say, out and about. Just yesterday, crutching out of a restaurant with Roix, three different people stopped me and asked, "What happened, are you okay?" Later another said, "I was on crutches for a month, don't worry, you'll get through it." My point is: These kinds of compassionate interruptions would never occur if they knew the enormity of my situation. When I respond, "Thank you, but I lost my leg a long time ago," I immediately see their surprise and I also hear their whispers, "Who would know? And . . . "She's smiling."

What we women of a certain age know is that challenges are not going to get any easier, but we remain determined to find ways to enjoy ourselves by maintaining momentum. When pain or illness shows up, we face it head-on. Despite the difficulties, the rewards of movement are to be savored and the blessings of good health are never to be taken for granted.

Chapter Six

Plastered

"FDR practiced diligently, but he hated the stiff-legged mechanical look the appliance gave him, the teetering sense of precarious balance, and above all the discomfort."

~ *The Roosevelts* by Peter Collier

I hope the following story will interest the reader as it's something not much talked about—prosthetics. Be it for women who've had breast cancer and chosen, for aesthetic reasons, to adjust to implants, or for me, a few years back at seventy-four, taking a chance on a computerized, hydraulic, prosthetic leg for comfort and the freedom to walk better.

It was March of 2017 when I made that decision.

Roix and I were driving south on the 408 Freeway to the small city of Torrance for a late afternoon appointment with Carlos, my prosthetist, who was going to fit me with a new, sophisticated, artificial leg.

Carlos has kept me walking on a variety of legs, since my amputation back in 1974. He was a protégé of Fred Karg, my first prosthetist, and today is considered one of the top prosthetists in the world for the fitting of legs for high level amputees.

During the drive, I was unusually quiet, filled with disturbing thoughts. Am I really a good candidate for this fantasy leg, considering my age and amputation? Can I truly learn to walk all over again on a totally unfamiliar leg?

Through the years, I've been fortunate to capitalize on the most advanced legs available to the radical amputee and I've done well, with few problems. I usually wear them out in two years' time, and Carlos loves to see me with my derelict legs. "It means you're using them!" he says with pride.

Near Torrance, I look so anxious, that Roix reaches over and pats my hand.

"Are you okay?" he asks, as he maneuvers the car in and out of the fast, aggressive traffic.

"I'm scared, Roix. God, I hate to admit it, but I am scared."

"That doesn't sound like you. What's up?"

"What if this high-tech leg won't work for me?"

"If it's too difficult, you'll just stay with your standard leg. Relax, everything's going to be fine," Roix adds, as he guides the car into the handicapped parking slot. He gets out and comes around to the passenger side and opens the door. As I step out, he offers me his arm.

"Thank you, dear, but quite frankly, I'd rather have your leg."

"That's the spirit!" Roix laughs.

Carlos, looking more like a handsome Latin athlete than a prosthetist, enthusiastically greets us at the entrance of the clinic, a concrete complex with narrow, cell-like rooms and floor to ceiling mirrors—nowhere to hide from my great loss. It's here where Carlos performs miracles on patients who have no other options because of their unique amputations.

"You're going to walk for the first time," Carlos beams, "without fear of your leg collapsing. Walk on all kinds of terrain—even down steep slopes, planting one foot in front of the other—not sideways as before. Your knee will get forty-five hours of power from a rechargeable Lithium battery. At night, you can plug it in right alongside your cell phone," he grins. "And listen, if you run out of juice when you're out and about, you just charge it up in your car's cigarette lighter."

"Wow! Well, let's get to it!"

"Hold on. First, I need to take you to the bars where I'll get you plastered!"

I burst out laughing. Carlos and I can always count on humor, no matter how sensitive the subject. He is my prosthetist, my pal, my confidant.

We went to the bars. Then I got plastered with wet towels dipped into a starch-like substance that Carlos stretched and bound around my hips to form a bucket-like device that later would connect to the artificial leg. While I balanced on one leg clutching the bar, Carlos spoke of another feature of the C-Leg.

"It's got a wireless, remote control to switch between modes of walking. Slow, medium and fast. This remote puts the convenience of mode switching in the palm of your hand."

"Oh, God, Roix is going to love to get his hand on that remote. He'll have me coming and going in every direction and speed just to make me crazy."

After standing on one leg for some time, hanging onto the bar for support, I sat down. "I need a break," I groaned. "Anything else you can tell me about this leg?"

"Well, another feature you'll really like is the standing mode. I know when you lecture you prefer to stand instead of sit, because of the positive impression it projects to your audience. Right?"

"Yes," I nod.

"But it's hard on your one leg. With this leg, you'll be able to lock the knee and stand secure yet relaxed, because you've taken the stress off your sound limb."

"Great," I say smiling.

"I'll need you to come back in the morning so I can attach the mold," he touches the bulky device that leans against the bar, "to the skeletal leg. And then, I'll need to make all the other necessary adjustments to the prosthesis."

The next day, when we entered the fitting room, we were greeted by a group of master prosthetic students who were there to observe the whole process. I was to be the guinea pig for that day and several days to come.

I was never concerned about showing off my abilities to

conform to a new leg, but today my performance would take on more meaning, as these young prosthetists learned how to accommodate other amputees with state-of-the-art legs. Also, I was thinking that my experience would help to teach the next generation about the realities of amputee situations, like the students who were watching. They have no life experience and I felt it was up to me to be willing to exhibit what it's really like. After all, what good is it if I don't pass it on?

Carlos sat on a small stool, ducking his head under and between the bars as he rolled around me with his tools in hand. He adjusted nuts and bolts on the skeletal leg then tossed the tools aside. Ever ready Roix, lying on the floor curious to see what was going on, picked up the tools when asked, and set them back into Carlos's hands. I was deeply touched by this heartwarming scene, watching my most loyal and trusted men trying to get me back on my feet.

The bucket was the most challenging feature of this apparatus and Carlos made every effort to give me a firm, comfortable fit. I remained quiet through the cutting, and the pinching of the hard bucket against my soft skin. I tried to be patient and disguise my fatigue at the physical effort of repeatedly being directed to sit, bend and walk, with the new, heavy equipment strapped to my body.

Meanwhile, the students stood, arms folded, mouths agape as they watched in amazement this demonstration of the raw, hard, yet great talent of Carlos Sambrano.

While I was slowly walking back and forth holding onto the bars, I overheard Carlos say something to the students that I hadn't known before and it shook me.

"The surgery could have killed her with so much blood loss. Mayo clinic was the only hospital at the time that could do this kind of surgery. They knew what they were doing when they amputated—leaving the crest of her hip for a possible fit into a bucket that would hold the leg in place. Back then we were in infancy. Very few hemi legs had been built yet. Even today, we've not perfected anything for the hip. What Lenor is wearing is the most advanced."

Being fitted for a computerized/hydraulic leg was a profound experience, to say the least. And yet, my resolve to make this bionic leg move, walk and come to life was absolute. Not only for me, but for all the amputees, of any age, who continually ask, "Lenor, are you still kickin'?"

Chapter Seven

Surviving Loss

"There is no strong person with an easy past. So wipe your tears, smile and keep moving. You are created strong enough for the cross to bear."

~ Meyo Adekoya

You don't get to be a woman of a certain age without having experienced grievous and heartbreaking losses. Before the age of forty, I had two major casualties: the loss of my leg to cancer and my husband, of seventeen years, leaving me for another woman. But I was determined not to let these losses cost me my dreams of living a full life. I succeeded because of my mindset: a grateful attitude for being cured of cancer and the determination to go it alone even as a single mom, with two young daughters, no financial support and a disability. Not to mention, entering the dating world wondering if a man could be attracted to me or even accept a woman with only one leg?

That was my situation when I moved into the Marina City Club. It all worked out, eventually, even the dating scene because of that sense of myself—fully confident that I was the same woman as before. Whenever I walked into a room, for example, I never thought of myself as an amputee. I exuded the impression that I was a total, consummate woman. I projected that image and I was successful.

As the years progressed, other losses come to mind. My daughter Christianna at fifteen was diagnosed with Bi-polar disorder. At the time, she was a popular, happy-go-lucky cheerleader who would never stop chattering. And then, one day, she became mute. Shockingly, after weeks of silence, she began to talk non-stop coupled with outrageous behavior.

My child's carefree innocence was destroyed by Bi-polar disease. My loss was to witness her sudden, interrupted life.

Christianna survived with the loving support of her family, proper medications and therapy. But, it was not, and still is not an easy journey. She's endured multiple hospitalizations and was given wrong medications that initiated wild hallucinations. Her classmates, not understanding her erratic conduct, constantly bullied her because she was either outrageously manic or flat and depressed. No one understood.

The miracle drug, lithium, finally stabilized her condition

and she went on to attend and graduate from San Diego State College, majoring in Early Childhood Development. Later, she married, and adopted two beautiful little sisters. Christianna's ability to live a normal life has been sustained because of her understanding of her disease, respecting the medications that she must take for the rest of her life, and her persistent dedication to her well-being. Just recently, she shared with me something I did not know.

"You know, Mom, when I was diagnosed as Bipolar, I was relieved because I was given a valid reason as to why I acted out in such monstrous ways."

Today, my darling first born has developed the strength and resilience to cope with this disorder and is living a full, happy life.

Another loss that many women of a certain age experience, is flagging energy—losing the stamina to do the physical things we used to do. This can be a fearful and daunting setback. For me, it's the lack of easy, quick movement that I really miss. So, I substitute.

. . . Like the other night when Roix called out for me to join him by the bonfire. I jumped up, in my heart and mind thinking, *I'll just run down to him!* But, instead, I had to slowly crutch outside, get on my ATV (Roix had already warmed up for me), and speed off. I'm always finding alternate ways that can offer me swift mobility.

As we age, I think we get better at facing and surviving loss. Not that it gets easier. It doesn't. Life can be a stern teacher, but the hardest deprivations we face are often the ones from which we learn the most.

Diane

"Switch the gears in your mind—then restart your motor."

———

My husband, Gordon, lost his zest for life when his health started to fail at eighty-seven years old. He became depressed, silent, and negative about everything. No more smiles. I struggled with the transition. I was no longer his partner; I was his caretaker. It became a major challenge for me to stay positive. I figured my positive energy would transfer to him, but after a while his negative energy transferred to me. I was strong for so long, but then I broke down!

My daughter urged me to take a break and she drove me up to a mountain resort for a few days of relaxation. Gordon went to his daughter's house for Father's Day. While there, he had a mini stroke. I raced down the mountain, feeling so bad for leaving him. Yet, our time apart had allowed me to take stock of our relationship. I realized how far apart we had grown and by distancing myself from him, I was able to renew my love in a deeper way than ever before. When we reunited, we both became loving and happy again. We even danced together to the song "Tennessee Whiskey," one of our favorites, for the last time.

At the age of eighty-nine, my dear husband bestowed upon me his beautiful, dimpled smile for the last time and passed away at home, surrounded by many friends and family. I had always wondered how people were able to handle the funerals of their loved ones so calmly, then I found out. The survivor drops into what I call a "No-Zone." During this time, you are in an emotional void, a timeless space where you just exist, where any next step is uncertain and unfathomable. Most of all, I felt guilty that I had not been a good caretaker, even though I know now I did my best. After Gordon's death, the ranch too lost its vitality! All the animals died except for one old dog and one cat. I was living on a "Ghost Ranch." All the sunshine had disappeared. I allowed myself to drift in the no-zone for several months, surrounded by my dream which was in decay.

However, as always, I was determined to go on! I will probably mourn my husband's death for a long time. But I have learned that in order to move on, you must switch the gears in your mind—then restart your motor. Gordon's ashes had been sitting on my bed stand for over a year. I had thought I might spread them on the golf course where he spent so many happy years, but it had closed down and gone back to nature. I discovered that it recently reopened as a recreational area. I called a girlfriend and a couple of Gordon's golfing buddies who had been with *him when he achieved a historic hole-in-one that won him a brand new car! I asked them to show me where the hole #3 had been. They joined me on the hike and we found it on top of a hill overlooking a little valley full of fall colors. My girlfriend brought out martinis with olives (Gordon's favorite drink) from her backpack. As I sprinkled his ashes over the spot where he won the car, his buddies reminisced about all of Gordon's funny jokes and dubious stories. We toasted to my husband's newfound freedom and sang his favorite song, "Green, Green grass of Home." I Love you, Gordon!*

Susan

"Giving attention and receiving attention are truly sacred acts."

———

My youngest, Kevin, was a Marine who served in Iraq, and later fought against ISIS in Syria. When he returned from those wars, his personal battles were just beginning. Though he tried to conquer his PTSD, and many tried to help him, he found no peace. He suffered terribly and, in the end, he took his own life. It has been a soul shattering experience for our family.

Though I experience grief in many guises daily, I strive to make a conscious effort to focus on gratitude. If I can move into a feeling of thankfulness, it's like a life preserver for me. I remember each day to be grateful that Kevin was my son and that we loved each other. I'm grateful for the lives he touched and the many lives he saved as a medic.

In those first days, after the terrible news that Kevin was gone from us forever, I was just numb, in shock. Eventually, I knew I had to find the "peace that surpasses all understanding," or I would go under and never find my way back. The single thought that kept coming was that I had to find something, anything, to be grateful for. It was like climbing out of the darkest abyss you can imagine. All I could think to do was to walk slowly around my house and begin to stick little notes on things that I could be grateful for—teapot, favorite pillow, ficus plant, woodstove, television, hot water, bathtub. If I could have stuck a label on the dog, I probably would have. It sounds nuts and I suppose it probably was, but as I wandered around so utterly shattered, those little labels reminded me that I was still here, and there were things that could comfort me if I let them. It truly gave me some sense of peace and grounding to be able to read each note out loud and say, 'Thank you for this beautiful teapot. Thank you for this cozy bed. Thank you for my comfortable chair.' Of course, I couldn't put labels on the trees and the river and the birds and the dog, but I mentally gave thanks for those things too as I went on my daily walks.

These days every breath is a prayer of thanksgiving and there really isn't much I take for granted anymore, especially time with loved ones and friends. Giving attention and receiving attention are truly sacred acts.

I've since come to understand that there really is no way around grief. You have to go through it and let it have its way with you my darlings. Just know that yes, it will get better, but know also that it will always be with you. Always. What we women of certain age learn is how to carry our grief and not let it carry us.

Cathy

"How I moved on."

———

I was raised in a small ranching town in California. My dad was a rancher; my mom a stay-at-home mother. We had love in that house with parents who loved my two sisters, me and my brother who was the youngest of the siblings. But when tragedy suddenly struck, sadness and despair ruled our happy home. No one is immune to tragedy or human suffering. It is how we accept and handle it that can make a difference in one's life.

It happened one afternoon when my brother, Greg, and husband, Franco, were playing golf. When they finished at the l9th hole, they got into my brother's new Porsche. Greg never came home and Franco was badly injured and in the hospital.

It was a horrific time for our family. My life was turned upside down. How could my life be happy after that, you ask? It took a while, and I still grieve for Greg but I have faith. Praying is a tool that I use every day. Supplication—the action of asking or begging for something passionately, heartfelt or humbly. I asked this of God. Please Lord, help me through this.

My mother passed away when she was only fifty-eight years old. I was filled with helpless, unbearable sorrow. How could I move on? I believe grief is always with you when you lose a loved one. My emotional pain was relieved by prayer, reading self-help books and staying busy.

Shelley

"I cannot accept that my losses will define me."

———

"Don't cry because it's over, smile because it happened." That was something someone said to me

early on after losing my husband. Indeed. But getting to that place takes some work.

What I have learned, since losing Alan, is that before you can smile, you HAVE to FIRST feel miserable and sorry for yourself. You must do the work of grief which is to acknowledge and FEEL how broken you are. No one likes feeling this intense pain and many try to suppress it or distract themselves from it, or even hurry it, but then it remains unprocessed and as a result, never goes away. It's like a dagger down your throat sometimes . . . in the first few months.

Like I said, regarding pain—no one wants any, but everybody gets some. Of course, you can't be miserable 100% of the time; you have to take breaks from misery, even while in the depths of it. Our hospice grief group facilitator gave a metaphor of grief in the first year as a bowling ball that you have to carry around with you. It's very heavy and you have to put it down and rest sometimes. Then you pick it up again . . . and go on . . . and on . . .

I realized yesterday that I'm thinking about Alan less and am not sure how to feel about that even though I know it's good in the long run. Then I remember he's only as far away as my next thoughts and that helps. What a process!

I have learned how ephemeral everything can feel—and maybe everything is. That whatever rug you are standing on can be pulled right out from under you with absolutely no warning. I felt like I got the cosmic bitch-slap! In the last few years, I have read about many women who lost husbands and then had multiple other rugs pulled out from under them. Many lack support networks and struggle alone as they face emotional distress and financial insecurity.

I know I am very fortunate because I have good friends and a strong support network and am financially secure. But life is all about change and even if life is good—it can change in an instant. So enjoy every good moment.

One of my fears was and still is that I won't experience the thrill of anticipation around holidays or planning events, the absolute joy of times shared, or the support and backing during the difficult times. Life shared with a loved one is a wonderful carousel that goes up and down, with different sights and different moments and always moves forward. I miss that sense of purpose, that feeling of looking and planning ahead, that sense of enjoyment of the moment and the sharing of memories and times gone by. With Alan, I experienced it all—past, present and future—and now I seem to be clinging to the past, only existing in the present and fearful of looking too far into what the future may hold.

I once felt fearless and embraced life—regardless of the situations. But now, I am often anxious, second-guessing and feeling like the ground is always shifting below me.

That being said, I just cannot accept that my losses will define me for the rest of my life. I will continue to try to be strong to look and move ahead when possible, and to believe that just as terrible unexpected things can happen in life—so can new and unexpected wonderful things!

I believe people and events enter our lives for reason and that we need to ride life's highway, the best way that we can . . . perhaps that's a little "Pollyanish" but for me, it's a better alternative than living forever in this grey, aimless, unemotional and monotone world.

I read about a rabbi recently who said that the most powerful one-line prayer he has ever read is: 'Let me not die while I am still alive.'

I would have never understood that prayer before losing Alan. I am starting to live again. I feel good when I am with caring friends. My husband would want me to enjoy what's left of my life. I am trying.

Diana

*"Mourning is constant, and it is occasional. It
hits hard, and it rides easy."*

———

I had thought mourning was active, something
you did: You threw your hair over your head and
keened. You wept and wore black clothes. Your heart
felt like stone, and there was an ache that hurt like a
knife. Nothing was untouched by the pall of grief.

Yes, but no. When Mike died, only six years after
we had met, leaving me to grapple with all the
could-have-beens that were now never-will-bes, I
found instead that mourning is like the sympathetic
nervous system; it is a thing of its own and doesn't
need my active participation. It is constant, and it is
occasional. It hits hard, and it rides easy.

Mike died eleven days before our first wedding
anniversary. I dreaded the mourning of that day,
so a few days before, I threw myself into a project
of putting together a wall of photographs of Mike,
during the time I knew him: choosing, printing,
framing, arranging, hanging. I had pictures from
many hikes: us at Mt. St. Helen's, at Crater Lake, in
the Dolomite Mountains of northern Italy, on the
green-sand beach in Hawaii, in the redwoods, at

the ocean. *There were honeymoon pictures from the northern California coast, touristy pictures from Aix-en-Provence and Croatia, pictures of Mike and me skiing. There were beautiful pictures from his illness, taken by a photographer who specializes in photographing people going through trauma, and from our stupendous wedding on the Applegate River. It was a wonderful project, bringing back memories that had me rejoicing, which, in the end, might be a part of mourning, too.*

Thinking it would mitigate mourning, I invited all the 150 wedding guests to light a candle for Mike and me in honor of our anniversary and to post a picture of it on Google Photos. All day, photos of candles were coming in. I felt surrounded by light and love. Candles were lit on the Applegate River, at the wedding site. Photos were taken of candles with the wedding invitation, with flowers, with paintings, with hands, and with special effects for Mike and me. I saw that doing this for us was a way for others to mourn Mike's passing while they also rejoiced in our life together.

On the day of the anniversary, three good friends came for lunch. They asked for stories about the photographs. We talked about the wedding, and they asked about Mike's three weeks on hospice and what that was like for me. It was good to talk about it. Grief is worse suffered in silence. They listened to all thirty-

five poems I had written during those weeks. Far from a day of mourning, it was a day of remembering and sharing and a spreading of love.

But maybe that is also what mourning is.

In general, the mornings are the worst—after I wake up from a night of dreams, mostly jumbled and confused, which I think is another kind of mourning. When I woke up the day after my anniversary feeling desolate and empty, I thought to hike the East Applegate Ridge Trail, that Mike and I had hiked with a small group of out-of-town wedding guests the day after our wedding. I imagined myself hiking with tears flowing, given the emotions attached to that trail, but once I started walking, my spirits lifted instead. As with the photographs and reading the poems, the memories became uplifting. The wildflowers were as beautiful this year as they had been the year before— Oregon sunshine, lomatia, Indian paintbrush, wild irises, and thirty-one other kinds—and I remembered how much my out-of-town guests had loved the beauty of our mountains, the views and the flowers. A breeze calmed my mind. Birds were a balm. Above all, there was the walking itself, in the woods, on the open hillsides, through the flowers. The day was succor.

Mourning is not an activity that precludes all others. Walking, writing, planting flowers, visiting friends, and recalling memories through tales and photographs are a part of mourning, which is like

the waves of the ocean: now crashing, now receding,
now flowing gently, now loud, now just a murmur.
Mourning is just a way of loving the one who is gone.

Missing You

I've found someone to hike with.
Yesterday, a friend cut firewood for me
And helped haul it into the woodshed.
There are a lot of other people in my yoga class,
And I'll still ski with the ski club.
My family will play games with me.
Any of my friends will, if I egg them on,
Spout off about politics.
But who's going to work crossword puzzles with me?
Who's going to hike Table Rock Mountain with me
once a week at dawn?
Who's going to go to the symphony with me?
Who's going to tease me about my lack of direction
Or the time I take to choose what to wear?
To whom will I read books?
Who will eat my marshmallow fudge brownies
And complicated recipes for tarts and ratatouille?
Who will lie with his arms around me at night

And share intimacies upon waking?
Who will build my garden beds?

Who will hike in Patagonia with me
Or the Grande Route in Switzerland?
Who will share with me the difficulties
Of running his business and other affairs
and listen to my own joys and woes?
Who will laugh with me?
Who will be my sympathetic ear?
Who will say, "I love you"?
Who will say, "I love you"?

Even if there were twenty people to do these twenty things
And a hundred more to do a hundred things more you did for me
They could never
Even cumulatively
Be for me
What you were.

It's so easy to pretend otherwise, but death isn't a rumor, it's a fact. It will come, sooner or later, expected or not. women of a certain age are keenly aware of this. We have all lost loved ones; friends, family, spouses. But none of us have given up, partly, I suppose, because life kept calling and we had no choice but to answer. We grieve, we long for things to have been different, but we don't focus on regret. We cherish the moments we shared and remind ourselves to appreciate all the ones we have left.

Chapter Eight

Seduction

"C'mon good girl, be bad."

~ Nicki Elson

"Has your sexual interest declined," I asked, of my ladies, "or have you been able to maintain an active sexual life?"

I've learned that these women have found a myriad of ways to cope with the time-induced changes of their sexual needs. Some ladies still desire a sexual relationship and must find new connections where they can, if they have lost their partners. Others no longer have any sexual appetite and or simply choose to close the chapter on that part of their lives entirely. But, in my opinion, we ladies who still desire sex can absolutely make it happen. If we have our health and a communicative, loving partner (a blessed bonus) and if we're not ashamed of our now aged forms and can throw body shaming judgments to abandon, we can continue to enjoy sex. Don't you think so?

Thankfully, Roix and I continue to enjoy each other sexually. Even though we have some of the physical symptoms of aging like arthritis or not being as graceful or agile as when we were young—these are all workable. And with my disability, I've learned how to adjust and come out "spinning like a top," I joke with my friends.

Many of the ladies say it's difficult to talk about sex with their partner and, worse, that it's embarrassing to describe what they desire. It's especially awkward, if they hadn't been clear over the years on the subject, because they felt shy, ashamed or even selfish to ask for something their partner never initiated—be it prejudices of our "era" or their men's reticence to the discussion or perhaps sexual repression. I suggest a woman, no matter what age, be bold and open those communication lines! You may be surprised that your partner has felt somewhat the same, unsure even curious about what his partner wishes sexually. He'll probably say, "Why in hell haven't we talked about this before?" I can honestly say that for Roix and me, sex has always been very pleasurable because we can talk about what we want, what we like, what's comfortable and what is uncomfortable.

Women also wonder, "How can I participate in sex if I'm embarrassed to even show my body? Hey, ladies, when the lights are out, we may feel much as we did years ago. And there's certainly ways to get into bed without parading around naked (for me it would be more like "hopping" around). No, you don't look like you used to, but if you still want to enjoy sex, let confidence guide you on how to get creative in revealing your body to your partner.

Now, one might think, how in the world does Lenor, with her amputation, feel or look sexy at her age? And with only one leg?! First of all, I learned a long time ago it's not so much what you look like, it's what you project. That's what others, but especially, your lover, responds to. So, I present myself not as disabled, but still BELIEVE myself to be sexy, attractive and desirable. How can my husband resist?

Just the other night, I was feeling in the mood. I took my time in preparing to seduce Roix, my husband. I encouraged him to sip a little wine while I lit the candles and turned on a Luis Miguel CD to set a romantic mood. I donned a black, long, negligee, combed my hair until it shined, and sprayed a touch of perfume in all the right places. I did not focus on my lost limb, instead I presented my best side first. Indeed, here is where, for me, a little imagination comes into play in the game of seduction.

I lay down close to him, and while I massaged his body with oil, I encouraged easy, silly, playful, sexual small talk. We often banter like this before, during or after making love, only adding to our joy in each other . . .

Like the time I was recuperating from shoulder surgery which made sex a little difficult. I had no issue telling Roix that I needed to pass; I had to do what was right for me. When I was feeling better, I decided it was time. . . . In the early morning light, I nudged my husband, "Honey." No response. He's hard of hearing, so I repeated, "Roix!"

He, finally, slowly, turned around to face me.

"You want to fool around?" I asked, with a provocative smile on my lips. Sleepy-eyed, he rubbed his eyes and blinked.

"What?" he shook his head, not hearing me correctly. "What? You want to buy that new refrigerator today?!"

I burst out laughing while playfully poking and tickling him.

He got the message . . . eventually! But, with an impish smile, he couldn't resist adding, under his breath "That ought to cool her down."

Sometimes men of a certain age have a difficult time achieving and maintaining an erection. Know that this is very hard for them to accept. So, you need to work past it, with care and zero judgement. Know that you can pleasure your partner by other means. And that is good for both your mojos!

To be touched, fondled, and kissed is more important to most men and women than the sex act itself. Maintaining physical closeness gives each other pleasure with or without engaging in intercourse. And there's always oral sex. I know, some women of our generation were brought up to believe that oral sex was unseemly. But, many of us found it was natural and healthy and sex became even more erotic and rewarding. Maybe I shouldn't go into it any further. My daughters will say, "Too much information, Mom!"

Another subject, ladies, is self-pleasuring—with vibrators! (I suspect my older ladies of a certain age will say "TMI!" but hear me out!) My opinion is, seriously, if there's not a man in the room and you're feeling aroused . . . why not use a vibrator to satisfy yourself? Life is short and contrary to the outdated beliefs we grew up with, self-pleasure doesn't only feel good, it is outright beneficial! Scientists tell us that orgasms trigger a surge of endorphins and oxytocins. Both can help with sleep, migraines and pain. After my surgery, I remember my pain was absolutely obliterated during sex! Laughing, I told my husband, "We're going to need sex all the time, if I want to avoid this awful pain." And my husband heartily agreed!

Ladies, if you haven't tried self-pleasuring, or have always been afraid to try it, don't be! There are massage type devices that you don't use internally. They are discreet and can almost always assure one or several climaxes. Give it a try! Us women of a certain age should live our lives to the fullest! I mean, really . . . what are we waiting for?!!

Okay, I'll refrain from supplying any more TMI and, instead, I'll add another anecdote on how goofy, sex communication can bring laughter into even dicey situations . . .

Last month, Roix and I were flying home from California at 12,000 feet above the smoke from one of the worst firestorms in the state's history. We were cruising parallel with the top of Mt. Shasta. The smoke was so thick, we could see nothing below. To lighten up the situation, I looked at Roix, who's lap was covered with maps and a tight seat belt. "Honey, how come we've never joined the mile-high club?" (The mile-high club is slang for people who have sex on board an aircraft at a mile high.) Roix, amused, played along, "Well, first you've got to find the co-ordinates, punch them in on the GPS, call ground control for approval, and then (pointing at his lap). "You must get clearance from the tower."

Diana

"I ease away from him so I can secretly sleep as though alone . . ."

It's not so much that I've grown resigned to sleeping alone, as that I like to sleep alone, even though I used to love to sleep entwined. (My first previous lover said that "Having me cuddle against him all night was like sleeping with a monkey on his back.") But now, when I sleep with the "new man" who is becoming more "significant" day by day, though not, or so I tell myself, I'm relieved to say night after night, I ease away from him so I can secretly sleep as though alone. That's fine in the queen-size bed in his house, but when we are in my narrower bed, I sleep dangerously close to the edge (metaphorical enough of being close to the edge of "relationship"). Metaphor aside, bodies sleeping close create heat. He told me once, when our feet touched in the night, that my body was like a furnace. (At that moment, yes. Hot, cold, hot, cold, hot, cold, is the rhythm of my nights.) When we are in bed together and those hot *flashes upswell, I can't just fling the covers aside in a pique of temper as I do when I sleep alone, taking the whole bed for splayed-out limbs, but in respect to my bedfellow, I uncover my naked body gently so as not to disturb the steadiness of his breath, which proves his sleep. When my body jolts awake at 3:00 a.m., I can't read till I grow sleepy, as I do when I sleep alone, making something useful of lying awake in those dark hours meant for dreams, but because turning on a light would disrupt his slumber, I stare into the dark, pleading with Morpheus to appear, revising the day's conversations to improve their endings, composing poems that evaporate when I fall sleep and don't recur when I wake again as he rises to answer the demands of his bladder. On the other hand, the talk in bed, before we drift into silence and his breathing deepens into sleep and I move surreptitiously to the edge of the bed, is one of the best parts of our intertwined lives, and sex (when it happens) is nice. Most of all, the drowsy conversations of morning as our bodies dawn into the awareness of a new day and of ourselves in it together, is an intimacy worth all the rest.*

Cynthia

"I think I just got my good sex early."

———

Well, between you and me, the best sex I ever had was with a dead man. Well, he wasn't dead then but is now. We were in our forties and dated for many years, and . . . boy! Was he inventive! How he got me to do so much I'll never know. And I loved the exploration he inspired! I can't bring myself to even suggest some of it with my current husband. But it was great then! Was it because I was younger? I don't think so. I think it was just that guy. He had a way of giving me permission to feel and do anything. Very glad I got lucky enough to have that experience. I bet some women never do. Sex now, is . . . well, just OK. I now only have it not too often—one or two times a month. I used to masturbate and exhaust myself with the shivers, but that doesn't seem to happen anymore. Maybe that's getting old. I don't talk about this with my husband. We just never have had that kind of conversation—in fact, really not any conversation about sex and love-making. Still holds true today. I think I just got my good sex early.

J.J.

"Sex needs sharing and trust."

———

As far as sex, my interest hasn't declined exactly. I love intimacy, but there needs to be stimulation with words and actions. I would very much like an intimate, romantic relationship coupled with a sincere friendship of sharing and trust. It is necessary for me to have a partner of mutual attraction and consciousness that I can be confident in and trust in order to keep intimate interest actively alive.

Susan

"I really just missed being held."

———

Romance? Sex? There was a period when I hadn't had either of those for over five years. Not that I was counting. After the last divorce, I did date a bit, but so many men in their later years can't perform sexually, so some just choose to abstain.

While I value my male friendships very much, during that five-year stretch, I still felt I was missing the intimacy of sex. Then I realized that what I really needed was just being held, hugged, and touched. Living alone now, days and days often pass when I never touch another human. It's something I took for granted—touch. Thank goodness for our pets, right? My little dog loves to cuddle, so at least I have the warmth of another being. In the end, I suppose I don't want to sleep with someone every night anyway, because frankly, I think most of us sleep much better alone. Between the snoring, the hot flashes and the other sleep disturbances we experience as we age, maybe we need to go back to the Victorian practice of having separate bedrooms altogether.

Anyway, what I have learned is that I will thrive with or without having an active sex life. as long as I can get a good night's sleep!

I say, we must get over the idea that it's inappropriate to enjoy the pleasures that our bodies can still offer. Some women even report that sex improves with age as we learn how to relax and get beyond our often puritan inhibitions. I don't know if it's a 'use it or lose it' proposition, but I do know that staying in sync with my libido has helped me continue to thrive. I believe it's perfectly healthy for women of a certain age to have an active sex life. Period!

Chapter Nine

Money, Money, Money

"Many people take no care of their money till they nearly come to the end of life, and others do just the same with their time."

~ Johann Wolfgang von Goethe

I've been rich and, I've been poor.

Rich, during the years I was married to the rancher and became a published author. Poor, when I lacked attention to the future and focused only on the moment.

Rich or poor, I always went my merry way as if I had money in the coffers. I don't know why I have this attitude. Perhaps, because my folks, who lived paycheck to paycheck, always worried about money. I vividly remember mom going over the bills each month with a troubled look on her face. "How in the world are we going to get by," she'd moan.

Since I was just a kid, I couldn't understand why mom was so sad and anxious while she signed checks the first of each month. We always paid the rent, food was on the table, gas in the car. So, all the worry and stress was for nothing, I thought, because life went on even with the little amount of money mom had in her bank account.

I also believed that if you had a job, money would never be a problem. So I always worked—beginning with teaching dancing lessons to the neighborhood kids in my parents' garage, squeezing oranges at the *Giant Orange* until my hands curled up at night into painful fists, and my favorite job, before going to college—switchboard telephone operator at Hills Brothers Coffee where I made it more fun by greeting the callers with different accents: Irish, Spanish and French. That job, however, didn't last long because my boss said he was tired of hearing, "Hey, John, *another* new operator?"

After hitch-hiking through Europe in the early sixties and settling in Rome, I made a little money dubbing B-rated movies. Upon returning home to the States, I was hired as a "gofer" for a fledgling movie production company in San Francisco. When they went bankrupt, I donned a white uniform, white nylons and white high heels and played at being a nurse for a while—you can imagine why that job didn't work out. And finally, before getting married, I landed a position at the Music Hyatt Theater papering the house—giving out free tickets when the celebrity couldn't draw an audience.

Once married to the rancher, I freelanced at modeling, writing a social column for the local newspaper and hosting a weekly radio show—none afforded much money. But it didn't matter because I loved performing and my husband took care of the family's finances.

After the publication of my first book, I was proud to earn and contribute money to the household. But, after the divorce, because of pride, I chose to leave with the children demanding no alimony, no half of home and ranch—nothing, only a small child support settlement. Suddenly, in my early forties, money became a huge issue for the first time in my life.

After the abrupt end of my marriage, my girls and I headed for Los Angeles and the Marina City Club where I used to stay while promoting my book. I had made the acquaintance of the Club's Chairman of the Board, Nick del Pesco, who would become a dear and lasting friend. He opened his arms to us offering a Promenade apartment overlooking the harbor—a far cry from the beet fields surrounding our old farmhouse. I accepted, not knowing how in the world I was ever going to pay the rent.

All I had going for me was my status as an author and the Southern California crowd believing I was a wealthy rancher's wife. It all worked for a while with me making excuses, partially true: "I'm expecting royalties . . . ," "I just sold the rights to my book in Holland and Portugal."

Our life at the marina came to a halt the day I found an eviction notice taped to the door of our apartment. I had just returned from a book tour in France where I had a best seller and was treated like a celebrity—but still there was no money coming in. I was stunned by the note; after all, I rationalized, I've been paying what little I could from my royalty checks— the rest of the money I used for living expenses. "How can this be? Can't they see I've been trying?"

Nick del Pesco once again came to the rescue. He convinced the board to write off the growing debt for the back rent.

"She has been our Club's biggest inspiration," he implored. "We comp Senators and wealthy businessmen, and what do we ever get in return? Lenor never refuses to offer advice or hope to our club members. She even gives our elderly members swimming lessons," he laughed.

Tearfully, I thanked Nick. But, knowing he couldn't protect me forever, I packed up and the girls and I drove to Santa Cruz, California, where we used to holiday long ago. My father signed for a rental but over the next few years, money continued to be a matter of concern.

Thankfully, royalties would trickle in from the U.S. and Europe, but not enough to sustain us. So, I found work at temporary agencies, masquerading as an assistant to a news-paper editor, an advertising agent for a real estate firm, and a cashier at a Cadillac dealership. My cane and limp were never questioned. Yet, it was obvious I had no skills, so I was regularly fired.

Christianna and Daniella were teenagers by then, so while going to school they always had part-time jobs; they chipped in together for living expenses and together we were able to get by.

We didn't have a lot of money, that's for sure, but we continued to live a good life.

The girls' new high school friends, boys and girls, thought of our home as their home; I reconnected with my old girlfriends from nearby Tracy and we met an array of new hippie friends from Big Sur who introduced us to a colorful, new, healthy way of life, with herbs, oils and Yoga. Weekends, we'd frolic on the beaches or in their large, makeshift cabins tucked high up in the Monterey mountains singing and dancing under the stars. Daniella, after falling in love with this lifestyle, announced she was now a "hippy," dyed her hair purple and became a vegetarian. Christianna held on to her "cheerleader" image.

Then Roix knocked on my door.

My husband has made me *rich* beyond my dreams—not monetarily—but by protecting me, providing for me, and loving me in this great adventure we share together called life.

Susan

*"What will I do if I can't support even my
most basic needs?"*

———

On the practical side, I hate worrying about running out of money. I never really took it seriously and now I'm paying the price for that. When I was working, I had more than enough, and believe me, I didn't squander my paychecks. But now, between the divorces, career changes, bad investments, natural disasters, and just plain stupidity, I find myself struggling.

It's a scary place to be at any stage of life, but as a woman of a certain age, it's a double whammy. What will I do if I can't support even my most basic needs? I've taken on numerous little jobs as often as I can to supplement the Social Security but it's a squeaker most months and I won't be able to keep this up indefinitely. As a result, I have learned to be a very careful shepherd of my meager resources. There is little to no room for unplanned emergencies, adventures, or spontaneous purchases. That sure as hell can take the fun out of life.

A couple of years back I took a trip to visit ten

different women friends that I've known for years. I was dismayed to discover that nine of the ten were struggling financially—NINE-OF-THE-TEN! On the one hand, it was reassuring to realize I wasn't the only one in this boat. On the other hand, what the hell is going on? I suppose part of the answer is that women typically earn 30% less than men over a lifetime, and we statistically outlive our male partners. This impacts our retirement and other benefits when we need them most. Social safety nets are waning and who wants to count on the government to look after us in our dotage anyway? Also, we don't have the kind of multi-generational living situations that our predecessors or other cultures have had so we can't count on family being able to take us in.

Gals, are we just fucked? I don't know what the answer is. I have hope that I'll continue to manage but there are days when I'm not feeling so strong.

Cynthia

Money is another worry I choose to ignore most of the time. Frankly, I'm amazed we managed to save as much as we did, but it's not nearly enough to get us thru the way we think. It used to make me crazy when

I was younger. God, if I lost a job, I was frantic, even though I lived like a queen. Now, I just figure if we run out of money, we'll find a way to get more. Can't we always work? Isn't someone always going to be impressed with our skills? Surely.

J.J.

———

Right now, money is important to me and there is no income. I never needed to be hugely rich but yes, money makes life more comfortable. And I like to be generous and enhance others with help when needed.

I enjoy life even though I have just become aware of serious financial concerns, I am very determined to manifest a positive outcome. I will be as happy as I choose to be.

Whether we have a little or a lot, money seems to be something many of us worry about. As women of a certain age we have had to learn how to keep our concerns around finances from overwhelming us and stealing our joy. We gals know there are plenty of ways to feel rich by indulging in small rewards like baking our favorite dessert, enjoying a beautiful sunset, using the good china for no particular reason, burning that scented candle you've been saving or buying a bouquet of fresh flowers for the table.

Getting fiscally literate might be a good idea too, in case you win the lotto, or, just in case you don't.

Chapter Ten

"Risk is just more life."

~ Jeremy Irons

One of the advantages of being a woman of a certain age is having the ability to look back at our lives and put the risks we have taken into context. I've been at risk for over forty years just stepping out of bed in the morning, with only one leg for support. Sometimes, I forget and start to walk as if I'm going to take a second step.

As I write this, I'm in Mexico where the floors are tile and slippery, stairs are cement with no railings and I must crutch through deep sand to get to the shoreline so I can dive in and swim. I have the added difficulty of my hand in a soft brace from recent surgery. But I come to Mexico, understanding my limits, because its rewards outweigh sitting at home contemplating whether or not I should participate in the things I enjoy. As the years unfold, I gain freedom by shunning fear.

With the passage of time, I find myself thinking about the many risks I've taken over the years but writing all of them down would try my readers' patience. So, I'll touch on the first wild adventure I experienced as a young woman and how it led me through these many years to understand that risk is just more life.

It was 1962.

I was a drama scholarship student at San Francisco State College when I found myself bored and so I quit. I'd decided I'd get the rest of my education hitch-hiking through Europe.

My travel mates were my sister, Diane and our best friend, Suellen—a redhead, a blond, and a brunette and we had a dream.

College dropouts, nineteen and twenty years old, we were totally naive about hitch-hiking through Europe. We never once thought about the dangers of getting into strange cars with strange men. Never considered the language barriers or foreign exchange rates. None of it mattered to fearless, small-town California girls. The journey would be worth the risks!

We were booked to debark in La Havre, France, but when we saw the emerald southern coast of Ireland and the ruins of ancient castles in the distance, we became enamored, jumped ship near the port of Cobh, tumbled into a small mail boat and landed on the shores of the seaside village of Cork.

The following morning, we began our journey in earnest,

walking past the outskirts of the village to a country road bordered by ancient, stone walls and covered with sweet smelling honeysuckle. We placed our three, overstuffed suitcases (we knew nothing about back-backs) upright beside us, pasted big smiles on our faces and stuck out our thumbs. In less than an hour, a line of police cars came speeding towards us. The lead car braked to a sudden stop, nearly causing a collision with the car behind. The police officer rolled down his side window.

"So, wher'you ladies be goin'?" he asked, in the lyrical, Irish dialect we came to love.

"Dublin."

"So, wh'y standin' there? Hop in ladies."

And so we did. For three months, through the British Isles and the Continent, we hopped in and out of laundry trucks, fancy cars and shrimp boats while experiencing the wonder of it all at every juncture.

On the road to Copenhagen we heard that Berlin was on "High Alert," after two East Berlin students had been caught climbing the Berlin Wall and were shot.

Sensing history in the making, we knew we had to be in Germany.

Before long, we were on the Autobahn, under a sign prohibiting hitch-hiking. We stuck out our thumbs and, literally, risked our lives flashing down cars speeding at over one hundred miles an hour.

No luck with cars so we flagged down a carrot truck. It was a tight squeeze in the cab commanded by a lecherous, crusty German. Our overloaded carrot truck swayed and lurched along the eastern occupied road. We stopped maybe three or four times at check points for our visa verifications. Along our route, we caught sight of German people clothed in their Sunday best standing on bridges tipping their hats and slowly waving as we passed under them. They had been abandoned, isolated in eastern Germany, since the end of World War Two.

We girls bounced up and down with the erratic movement of the heavy truck, and our driver decided to take advantage of our proximity and began to brush his hand up and down Diane's leg every time he shifted gears.

Diane became very upset and began to sing in a high operatic voice, "Loo . . . k! L . . . k what this guy is d . . . oing!"

Why are you singing? I shouted.

"This guy probably speaks a little Eng . . . lish, and I don't want to make him maaaaaaad!"

To amuse Diane, Sue and I sang along, "Don't woooorry, he doesn't speak Eng . . . lish!"

"I'm out of here, girls, tell this guy to stop the truck! NOOOOOOOOOOW!"

"Calm down, Diane, we can't get out onto this roa . . . d!"

"Oh god, his ha . . . nnnnd is on my thi . . . hhhh . . . !"

Unaffected by our operatic performance, the German's grubby hand, continued to travel further up Diane's leg.

"I'm jumping out of this truck now . . . get out of the way . . . !"

"Please . . . put up with it just a little lonnnn . . . ger, we'll be in Berlin . . . soon!"

Diane, near hysteria, jumped on top of Sue and me,

struggling to get away from the German's paws.

A soon as we pulled into the outskirts of Berlin, Diane now on Sue's lap, screamed at the guy to stop the truck.

Surprisingly, he geared down and brought the truck to an abrupt halt. We girls hurriedly opened the door and dropped to the ground. Diane first then Sue toppling behind me. We grabbed our things from the back of the truck and started walking. As the German drove off, he shouted in perfect English, "Have a good day, ladies!"

We were soon to see what was left of East Berlin by way of an invitation from a couple of Princeton students, Chad and Sterling, whom we met at our guest house and were working at the American Embassy.

The train stopped at Checkpoint Charlie, the only entry into East Berlin. We were a little frightened to see soldiers with machine guns, locked and loaded staring down at us from gray, rickety, wooden towers that guarded the Berlin Wall. Chad reminded us that the Wall had been erected only a year before, August 13, 1961. Since then not many people had been allowed in.

"Our passports are in order, let's go," Sterling whispered.

We stepped out of the shabby checkpoint building and stood in awe as we faced the still standing Brandenburg Gate, the entrance to *Unter den Linden*—once the most fashionable boulevard in all of Europe.

"We'll stay close together," Chad instructed quietly.

We walked under the majestic Brandenburg Gate and down the broad avenue and were shocked when we set eyes on the ruins of half the city of Berlin. To suddenly enter a city that appeared to be razed only yesterday by American bombers was surreal. The Cathedral was destroyed. The Kaiser's residence and Humboldt University were obliterated. Only small hand-painted signs stuck out from the rubble: "Under Reconstruction—1944."

The East Berliners were dressed in well-preserved fashions of the late thirties and early forties but wore desperation on their faces as they furtively moved across the streets and conversed in hushed tones. The backsides of apartment buildings were propped up like Hollywood sets with no infrastructure, no tenants. Our hearts broke when we internalized the devastation of war and prayed our generation would never be involved in another war which was nothing less than innocent, wishful thinking.

We left Germany and headed for Austria. In route, we had to hitchhike through the Bavarian Alps which were a problem as only tiny Volkswagens and Renaults whizzed by us on the curvy roads. So, we came up with a plan: one of us would stand on the side of the road and two of us would hide in the bushes. Sue, tall, beautiful, and blond, was our natural pick to brave it alone. Soon a Fiat came barreling up the road and Sue brought the pocket-size car to a prompt halt. The excited Italian driver opened the passenger door. Sue threw her suitcase on the floorboard, jumped in while splitting the air with a piercing whistle—our signal to come out of hiding and pile into the back seat.

"*Grazie, Grazie,*" we repeated as we tried to cram our suitcases and butts into the back seat. The driver frantically shook his head, "*Ma, ma, he pensato che era solamente una ragazza*, ('But, but I thought it was only one girl!')." "*Grazie, Grazie,*" we repeated, as we slammed the door shut.

Once in Rome, Diane, due back at her job in the states, returned home, but Sue and I decided we didn't want to go home. We, innocently, thought that all we had to do was present ourselves at the American Embassy and they'd find us jobs. It didn't happen.

After weeks of looking for work, Sue landed a job with an American company and I nailed an audition and got the call to dub Italian movies into English.

A primitive apartment in *Trastevere*, the oldest part of Rome, was our first home. Our shuttered windows looked out at lines of washing hanging across narrow cobblestone streets. We gobbled up the city's history riding on the back of Vespa scooters while local students weaved their stories about one ancient monument after another.

I became a bohemian to the core, speaking and looking Italian. I absorbed the culture and felt one with it. I turned twenty-one and became my own person and thought I would never return to the States. But after experiencing a cold winter with no heat, no warm clothes, little money, and my family and boyfriend Joe pressing me to return, I booked passage home. Sue never returned; she married a handsome stunt director, had four children and today lives in a picturesque village outside Rome.

Looking back, hitch-hiking through Europe, and deciding to live in Rome with no financial resources, no family or friends was probably riskier than we realized, but we never gave it a second thought. Why? Was it because we were young and naive? Or intrepid and strong? In any case, I'm glad we did it.

Through the years, because of that long-ago hitch-hiking trek, I've continued to take risks, sometimes out of necessity and other times for the thrill. However, in 1985, a trip to Las Padres Island, Mexico, was not for the excitement but for the money. Royalties were slow coming in and I was desperate to put food on the table and pay rent. A longtime friend offered to help me out. All I had to do was drive a car across the Mexican border. He flew me to Mexico where I was to pick up a car and after crossing the border, I was to drive to San Antonio, Texas, where we would meet up and I would be paid.

It was a steaming hot day when I approached the Mexican border. I gripped the steering wheel of the rented 1975 Pontiac Granville and tried to remain calm and look casual. Ahead of me, police were at the entrance carrying assault rifles and holding ferocious dogs in check with chains. Slowing down, I looked in the mirror and applied scarlet lipstick. A guard waved me down. My heart pounding, I held my breath, smiled and began to brake. However, the guard didn't stop me, he just motioned me through. Oh my God, how did I find myself in this situation, with marijuana hidden in my leg and in the bowels of the car? Well, it paid the rent.

Today, paying no attention to age, I continue to seek new thrills—not criminal, mind you but a little daring. Like when I'm in Mexico, and I want to swim in the ocean. I alert the life guards that I'm ready to hop on their Floating Chair with its balloon tires. They then carry me past the breakers to where I'm able to jump off the chair and swim out to sea towards the buoys where Roix awaits. The life guards, arms crossed, anxiously wait for me to return. Or how about just last weekend riding the rapids of the Rogue River.

"I bet you're the only seventy-nine-year-old grandma in the whole world with one leg paddling a raft down a river with your grandkids," my grandson, Elliott laughed.

"Perhaps, not the whole world, darling."

Diana

"We were on our own for handling any emergency until help arrived."

———

Before leaving for a three-day, hut-to-hut, cross-country ski trip in the Central Oregon Cascades in February 2019, my ski friend, Holly, and I were relieved to see, on the web site, that two other people would be skiing with us. If we ran into difficulty, four people could help each other better than two.

The First Day, 6 miles

We met those two skiers, Rhode Islanders, Katie and Emily, at the Three Creeks Sno-Park. They were as glad to see us as we were them. I was the most relieved to have the other three, as I was by far the oldest.

In a building at the Sno-Park, the outfitters gave us an orientation. We would be skiing a total of twenty-two miles at an average elevation of 6,500 feet. We were on our own for handling any emergency until help arrived. This was not a trip for beginners. The challenge would lie in variable snow conditions—possibly ice—and long distances. If there were a snowfall, we would be breaking trail. We would be alone in the backcountry. We were given maps, a GPS, and an emergency camping shelter. We carried our own sleeping bags and personal items. Food and cooking equipment were in the huts.

Orientation over, the shuttle took us to Dutchman's Flat, on Mt. Bachelor. We put on our skis, took a deep breath, and pushed off. Almost immediately, we were in trouble: ski tracks went up the mountain and, more flatly, ahead. Which way to go? Knowing we had to gain altitude, we followed the upward tracks, but Holly and I quickly realized that only skiers with skins on their skis could have gone that way. A closer look at the map showed us that we should keep to the level trail.

Katie and Emily laughed. "What do we know?" they said. "We thought this was cross-country skiing in Oregon!"

From there we skied more gradually, and therefore

more sensibly, up the mountain. The snow was deep, the skiing superb, the woods and hills beautiful in their deep snowcoat.

We skied for hours, deeper and deeper into the wilderness. We took turns breaking trail. We took strenuous herringbone steps up one hill after another, the last being the steepest, longest, and most exhausting hill I had ever herringboned up. We sidestepped up other hills. We skied down difficult slopes that felled everyone but Katie. As the day wore on, I began to tire. I fell again. I admitted to being tired. Everyone was tired. When we got to the Happy Valley Nordic Hut (altitude: 6,489 feet), I sank into a chair with relief, so did everyone else.

Recovery was quick. Soon, we were all doing chores—starting the fire in the wood stove, scooping snow into pots to melt for water, laying our sleeping bags on the mattresses in the upper bunks, getting food from the cabinet for our pasta dinner, heating water, setting the table.

Over dinner we learned a little more about each other: that Emily (27) was a high school science teacher, that Katie (28) was a physician's assistant in an emergency room, that Holly (58) was, as I already knew, a certified fiduciary, that I (74) was getting married in May. We played Bananagrams, then went to bed early.

The wind howled all night. Snow fell voluptuously,

in sparkling crystals that gleamed in our headlamps when we went to the outhouse during the night.

The Second Day—7 miles

The world was beautiful in its new twelve-inch layer of snow. We took turns breaking trail. The skiing was superb, beginning with a long downslope with a lapis lazuli sky to our left, then offering roller-coaster skiing and then a series of switchbacks, zigzagging up the mountain. At the top, we stood on our skis for a few minutes to eat a snack, then pushed off again.

Our hearts were singing. Everything was so beautiful—the various skies, from blue to black to roiling grays, the deep soft snow, the rhythm of skiing, the forests we skied through, the deep solitude. It was seven or eight gorgeous miles to Lone Wolf Hut (altitude: 6,451 feet). We arrived in fine spirits and, as before, set to the chores. Dinner that night was rice and beans.

The Third Day—6 miles

Again, about a foot of snow fell overnight. The skiing would, again, be superb.

I awoke early, hoping to start the fire and warm the hut before the others were awake, but Katie was up shortly after me. As I was stoking the fire, she called me to the window, and we watched together as a dark brown mink scooted into view, then leapt away through the snow.

On this day, we descended more than 1000 feet. The trail was just as beautiful as on the first two days. The clouds lifted at last to reveal Cascade peaks. We skied through a burned-out forest in which every tree was painted with ice crystals, and the forest, whether close-up as we skied through it or as a panorama from the top of a hill, was utterly beautiful.

We skied into the Three Creeks Sno-Park at 1:00, exhilarated and thrilled. It had been a wonderful trip— three days of skiing as the only way to get anywhere— an accomplishment for skill, a challenge for trail-finding, an entrance into an enchanted world of snow and solitude and a camaraderie of deep, though new, friendships, with people who flowed easily into rhythms of work, conversation, and shared physical exertion. We had started the trip as strangers; we ended as close friends. We hugged each other tightly as we parted.

"See you next year," I said to Emily and Katie, and they said, "Yes. We'll be here."

The next week, two skiers on the same route got lost and spent the night without shelter before they were rescued. One of them died in the hospital.

Susan

*"Fire burned over us and we prayed for
our very lives."*

———

*Well, I've certainly done some stupid stuff, as
have we all. Not that all risks are by definition life-
threatening, but don't you sometimes wonder how it
is that we've lived through some of the risks we've
taken?*

*Really, what could I have been thinking when I
decided to move off-grid, to a tiny cabin at the end
of ten miles of nearly impassable, dirt road? I was
not thinking that I'd someday be trapped up on that
mountain by a raging forest fire and end up running
for my life, jumping in a pond with my two dogs
and the neighbors twelve-year-old son while the fire
burned over us and we prayed for our very lives. No, I
wasn't thinking that.*

*But should I have never gone to live off-grid and
experience the absolute splendor of living in intimate
close harmony with nature? I would not trade those
years up on that mountain for anything. It was the
thrill of my life. Would I go back now? Nope. It was
too hard and too isolated, but I'm so very glad I had
that experience.*

As we age, I think we get more and more risk averse, maybe for some very good reasons but I don't want to just give in to fear and play it safe for the rest of my time. Where's the fun in that?

Lately, I have trouble driving at night. That doesn't mean I can't drive at night. It just means I have to be more careful if I'm out late.

I try to greet every new day as a welcome adventure and take my daily risk-taking in stride. Is it a risk to start a new writing project? What if I fail? What if I spend weeks or months working on something and it goes nowhere? Is it a risk to crutch out to the pool and climb in? Sure, I could fall. In the real world, just driving down the freeway has an element of risk, but if you want to get anywhere . . .

In my view, the risk of doing nothing, is too great. Because it's essential to our well-being, we women of a certain age take the risk of keeping our hearts and minds open, expanding our boundaries, and reaching for new experiences. The rewards inevitably outweigh the risks.

Chapter Eleven

Friendship

"You drink too much. You cuss too much. You have no morals. You're everything I ever wanted in a friend."

~ Anonymous

One of my questions to the ladies was about relationships with friends. Through the years, I've chosen friends, as opposed to doctors, therapists or psychiatrists, because they've guided me, loved me and even hassled me—for no charge.

Some of the major regret I've had in life is giving up on a friendship because of a minor or even major misunderstanding. I miss these friends to this day and wish I could say I'm sorry but I can't even remember what we argued about.

Now, I cherish old friends and, of course, making new friends. I have a quirky little story about Susan, my principal editor, whose narrative is also included in this book, and the friendship we've enjoyed for over twenty-five years.

Susan and I met in 1991 shortly after Roix and I had moved to Rogue River, Oregon, where we soon discovered that our neighbors were mountain people, leery of city folk, especially Californians. I suffered a bit of culture shock, missing the drop-in visits of my California pals over wine and talk of travel, books, music, and theater. The Oregon neighbors, however, gave us a cold reception and it wasn't likely they would take us up on an invitation to visit, much less enjoy chatting about a newly discovered novel over a cocktail.

Then I met you, Susan. Remember that day?

Yes, I certainly do, Lenor. I was dressed in a pair of dirty overalls, no make-up, grubby flannel shirt and rubber boots, gardening in the front yard of my cabin when I heard the approach of a four-wheel ATV on the gravel road. Imagine my shock when I looked up and saw you pull up to my gate dressed in a black, lacy cover-up, billowing out behind your bright red ATV. Your hair was swept up in an elegant chignon and you wore dangling earrings, lipstick and makeup. "Hello," you said, "I'm your neighbor."

Well, I was feeling a little lonely and disorientated, myself, having recently moved from Seattle. On top of that, I had heard some disturbing descriptions of an author who lived down the road. My neighbors said she was an amputee whose husband had to strap her onto an ATV so she could ride around the property. I must admit, the author part interested me but the rest sounded a bit grim. So, for a while I wasn't too anxious to run over and make contact with this new neighbor.

Then there you were in the flesh, asking me if I'd like to join you at the creek for a cocktail. "I have a pitcher of martinis in the cooler," you giggled. "Hop on and I'll give you a lift."

Your invitation flowed with an effortless grace that for a moment I was in disbelief at such an unlikely apparition there at my gate. I felt like throwing myself on the ground at your feet and crying "Oh thank God! Thank God you've come!" I charged out the gate, hopped on the back of your ATV and spent a delightful afternoon sitting by the creek chatting over a shaker of perfectly chilled martinis. It was heaven.

Indeed, it was. And, to think that an unscheduled stop on my ATV at an unknown gate, I'd find Susan who became not only a dear friend but a trusted workmate helping me edit and promote my second and third books. I relish her quiet intellect, joy of nature, and interest in everything from gardening to volunteering in the community to always being a phone call away when needed for advice or comfort.

Susan lost her son, Kevin, this year to suicide. I was in Mexico when I got the news. That night with tears and hearts full of anguish, Roix and I stood on the dock as the sun set, and raised a toast to Kevin, a wonderful, courageous young man who fought in wars in far off countries with honor. I can't imagine the agony of losing a child this way, but again, my friend is finding a way to regain her sense of self.

There have been other friends who've encouraged, sustained, counseled and humored me over the years. Their friendship has helped me define myself and I can't imagine my life without them. Many have given time and effort to contribute to this book, simply because I asked. They cheered me on and have helped realize it's completion.

Cynthia

"My friend's death—the void will never be filled."

Most of my long-term friendships are via my iPhone. I do miss getting together regularly in person, but that just can't be with our traveling lifestyle. I'm lucky that several key friends spend their vacations visiting us—for instance, my friends of forty years, who got engaged on our balcony when we lived in La Jolla, CA, and whose wedding we were in, have rented a cottage on an island where we'll be to celebrate their twenty-fifth anniversary. Sweet memories to be made . . .

My dearest and longtime friend died seven years ago, and my heart still breaks when I find myself thinking, OK, Judith, what would you say about this? That void will never be filled, but I still spend hours reading her myriad emails from days gone by. They make me smile and sometimes even laugh out loud. I love sharing them with her family every once in a while, just for the heck of it. They appreciate it too. Judith was and always will be my inspiration. She raised five kids to my two, and our constant remark, "This fifteen minutes everything is fine," (or not), was paired with our agreement that only one of us could have a crisis at a time! For much of the years a long-distance friendship, we often orchestrated 1,000-mile road trips just to spend time together. I highly recommend it to everyone with a dear friend!

Susan

"Don't let long-time friendships languish."

———

When Lenor asked me to write about being a women of a certain age, I thought this was damn funny because of all the women I know, she seems the least subject to the whims of Father Time. She has been, and remains one of the most inspiring, vital and dynamic women I have ever known, and I feel so lucky to have her and Roix in my life.

I've been lucky to have an amazing cadre of friends. These people have been there for me when the bottom fell out, after the forest fire took my home, after my divorces, after each of my parents passed, and again when my son took his life. Never underestimate the value of your friendships when the shit hits the fan. I think there is an Irish saying about how friendships double our joys and halves our sorrow.

I've tried very hard not to let my long-time friendships languish, despite the distances and changes. I regularly reach out and make efforts to stay in touch. We all have lives and demands that garner our attention and keep us in our respective bubbles. But my friends are very dear to me and I want them to know it even it's just to send a birthday card or talk on the phone a couple times a year.

I read somewhere that having good friends is way up on the list of things that help us live long and healthy lives. I'm sure that's true.

Melinda

"I thought of how I'd let my fear of aging overtake me until I met a friend . . ."

———

I have always learned from friends and they invariably lift my spirits. A few years back, Lenor was hosting our writers group of five women friends who had been meeting for ten years. I was ready for a change, and something happened that weekend that would bring the change I needed.

As we sat by the creek on her thirty-acre property, under the oak trees, I listened to Lenor read from the memoir she was working on. Hearing her describe the heart-wrenching story of losing her leg and half her hip to cancer, then being left with two children by a husband incapable of coping with her condition, touched me deeply. Lenor had risen out of the ashes, forged ahead with supernatural determination and wrote a best seller about her experience.

I'd been writing about my bipolar, drug-addicted daughter and had been on a roller coaster coping with her addiction followed by recovery. I lived in fear of what could happen to her. It had worn me out, body and soul, and I felt that I was aging beyond my years. Sixty felt like eighty.

I had hopes that by writing about my daughter, I could show other mothers that they're not alone. Hearing the story of Lenor's publishing journey convinced me even more that, I too, could use my painful experience to help others.

As I watched the creek tumbling over rocks, I thought of how I'd let my fear of aging overtake me, wear me out and suck my vitality and spirit dry.

I was determined to discover Lenor's secret. So, I asked her, "How have you stayed so happy all these years?"

She flashed her bright smile, brushed back her velvet brown hair, "That's why I'm writing this book, my dear," she said.

After hearing her chapters depicting life after her amputation and the collapse of her marriage, I thought how I might have wanted to curl up in a ball and die. But she had kept moving forward. She had faith in herself. She had gratitude, focused on life's assets, not deficits. She never talked about aging the way I had. She would only mention how grateful she was that she was able to get around the way she did, that she had the energy to keep up with her grandchildren.

I noticed that whenever anything wasn't always what Lenor had planned, she'd say, "Not a problem." Recently, she had gotten her new prosthetic leg and was having trouble adjusting to it. She didn't complain, she just said "I just have to get used to it," which she did eventually.

Positivity is the name of her game, and I wanted to be on her team. This, I decided, could not occur without four very important components: Self-esteem. Self-love. Self-care and Selflessness. I was convinced that I, too, could make the choice to be happy. When I changed the way I looked at aging, my attitude toward it would change. It was my decision. And my decision would become embracing my age, being grateful that I'm still here, looking not at the deficits but at the assets, as Lenor had done.

Diane H.

"Fate has a funny way of bringing people together."

———

At eighty, I am living on my ranch with friends of all ages (the key to enjoying life), throwing parties, hiking, biking and dancing at all the wonderful local festivals throughout the summer and fall. Most importantly, in keeping with my ageless entrepreneurial spirit, I have turned my beloved horse ranch into the perfect Air BnB/Horse Motel. Once again, the ranch is infused with activity and I get to play hostess and enjoy the *many interesting guests who I now consider friends.*

Fate has a funny way of bringing people who become friends that you need into your life. I call them my "Grey-haired Angels," and they became part of my journey when I rented them a couple of spaces to stay on the ranch. One is a sixty-six-year-old respiratory therapist. The other is age eighty-two, a retired contractor. Both are talented musicians who help around the ranch, putting up new fencing, fixing barns, and whatever needs to be done. They made it possible for me to get the ranch bustling again, with horses, sheep, chickens, cats and dogs. This summer at the pool has been wonderful. The three of us have been dancing, singing and swimming, with friends coming to join us. Only a few at a time and socially distanced of course! We were mentioning the other night, how wonderful it was to be marooned at Rustic Ranch Retreat during the pandemic!

Diana C.

"Friendship with my grand-daughter is imaginative, exhausting and free-spirited."

———

I am so sore! I have aches and pains, bruises and bumps, screaming stomach muscles.

What was I thinking, playing with my grand-daughter as though I were her nine-year-old friend instead of her grandmother friend?

It was so hot while I was visiting that week that my granddaughter asked to play in the sprinkler. She ran through it, again and again, urging me to join her, but, really, I'm beyond the age of playing in sprinklers, even with as good a friend as my granddaughter. Still, I was tempted just to get wet, so I went inside and put on my bathing suit. When I came back out, my son had spread a long sheet of black plastic down a steep slope on the lawn, with some rubber mats under it and the sprinkler at its top for a slip-n-slide. My granddaughter was already sliding joyously down the hill.

"Come on, Amma Dee!" she yelled. "You try it. Come on."

Well, I mean, how undignified could I get? Sliding down a hill at my age? No, no, I said. But I did sit at the top and tease her with pretend pushes as she tried to crawl up the plastic. "I'm coming up the black river," she would say, making her way up the slippery route, and then, within my reach: "Oh, no! It's the Amma-Dee squid!" and I would lunge at her, and she would go sliding down with squeals and laughter.

"Come on, Amma Dee. You do it." Then, when I wouldn't: "Bad Granny!" Bad Granny! Bad Granny! In the first place, I am not Granny. I'm Amma Dee. And I

144

couldn't bear being a bad grandmother.

That did it. Down I went, on my bum. She was delighted, and I had to admit, it was fun, so I went down again, but this time, I fell over a bit and slid down on my hip. I went really fast! And it was really, really fun.

For the next three hours, she and I played on the slip-n-slide. We slid down the slope one after the other, convulsing in laughter at the bottom. I was getting plenty of speed by sliding on my hip, even flying past the end of the plastic, stopping only when I hit the grass. When I stood up, my legs were flecked with grass cuttings.

Once, when I stood up after my slide, still on the plastic, my feet slipped out from under me, and I fell— boom!—on my bum. (It's a hard way to learn that I don't have osteoporosis, I thought ruefully.) Another time, I slipped unexpectedly and crashed into my granddaughter, both of us tumbling down. Sometimes, when I veered off track in my uncontrollable slide, I hit the dry part of the plastic, which was very hot. I screeched the rest of the way down.

Besides "Amma-Dee Squid," we played "taxi:" when we landed at the bottom, my granddaughter would start crawling back up the hill, with me hanging on to her ankle. She was the taxi, pulling me up the hill, except, of course, she wasn't strong enough to pull me up, so really, I was hanging onto her ankle and pulling myself up with my elbows and thighs. But the plastic was very slippery, and I really did need her nine-year-old's strength as well as all the strength I had to crawl on my stomach up a steep hill of wet plastic. We made incremental progress, slipping backward, then heaving forward again. I kept putting my head down to rest, saying, "I can't. I can't," and then gathering energy for another pull until finally, every time, we made it to the top, dissolving again into giggles.

We screeched and yelled and laughed. We slid down, out of control. We pulled ourselves up again. It's no wonder I feel like I've been beaten. Good Lord, I'm almost seventy-three years old. Don't I know better than to be throwing myself around like a nine-year-old?

It was wonderful. It was imaginative and exhausting and free-spirited. My granddaughter loved it. I loved it. And when I left the house to catch the ferry, the beginning of the journey home, she came running from the house, threw her arms around me, and gave me another long, tight hug. Every bump, bruise, ache, and pain I have now was worth that moment.

Friendships give us perspective. New friends offer a chance to look at life from a new angle. Old friends can be like family, letting us shine our light in comfortable conversation, sharing laughter, memories, and nurturing companionship.

New friends can challenge our views and urge us to take steps towards change or introduce us to unfamiliar subjects and experiences. Old friends help us remember our accomplishments and remind us that we've survived everything we've been through, cheering us on and including us in their adventures.

Chapter Twelve

Chasing Dreams

"If you choose anything in life, choose the things that get you excited about living."

~ Shannon Alder

Throughout my life, I'm glad that I've been willing to entertain surprising opportunities and stay open to unexpected possibilities. Too often, we tend to get stuck in ruts if we're not careful and live lives that are just OK. Okay is safe and comfortable but having the passion to chase a dream is awesome whatever your age.

I've pursued many dreams—some realized; others not. After my surgery, I began to have even bigger aspirations, wanting to prove to myself that I could still dream regardless of my physical circumstances or my age.

Writing my autobiography, with not much experience in writing, producing fashion shows, hosting a radio show, writing a second book and now my third—all could have been mere fantasies. Instead, by not holding back but unleashing my desires, I was able to accomplish much of what I had planned.

One of the wackiest dreams I was to ever follow was a television show called *Dr. Sickmund Fred*.

I was in my late forties living in Santa Cruz, California, trying to stich my life together after my divorce, when I got a call one afternoon from Dr. David Zuccolotto, a local psychologist and talented cartoonist.

"I read your book *One Step at a Time*," he said, "and it inspired me with an idea for a television sitcom that would involve you and a cartoon character as your therapist."

I was a little confused but intrigued. When I quizzed David, I learned he'd written a book, *The Truth About Psychology—Or Pretty Damn Close—Dr. Sickmund Fred's Case Notes and Diary*, which featured a cartoon therapist who pokes fun at screwball psychologists and their wacky clients. Always open to a project that might include *"moi,"* I invited David to my apartment to hear more about his idea.

He arrived brimming with enthusiasm.

"This is a true story, Lenor," he began. "It's your story, except for a magical, surprise ending. It's called, *Lenor's Place, With Dr. Sickmund Fred*."

"Go on . . . "

"Right." Pause. "A farmer's wife from the wheat fields of Central California arrives on the golden beaches of Malibu. She's forty years old, looks thirty, has lost her leg in a rodeo accident and turned the tragedy into a best-selling autobiography. Her success lands her a membership at Beverly Dunes, a private, beach front condominium."

"Uh-hum . . ." I arch my eyebrow.

David accelerates his delivery.

"Suddenly single, with two teenage daughters, her life is all about success, parties, and non-stop social activity. Yet, she sees the shadows behind the bright lights of her popularity. Royalties from her book sales are never consistent. Single life is overrated, and parenthood is a constant challenge, with her girls ripe for Hollywood glitz and L.A. style."

"Continue," I say, my curiosity aroused.

"The twist develops from the comic strip *Dr. Sickmund Fred* that's in the newspaper delivered each morning to the residents of Beverly Dunes. Dr. Sickmund is a kooky, loveable cartoon psychologist with a unique and witty perspective on life. His theory: Life is simple; you pay for fifty years of therapy—then you die. He shares an office with his outlandish and sometimes troublesome sea lion, Faust, and his Jewish secretary, Estelle."

David thrusts his book onto my lap and sits down beside me.

"Here, take a look at these comic strips; it'll give you an idea of Sickmund's humor."

In the first clip, Dr. Sickmund and Faust lie on the office floor staring into one another's eyes. Dr. Sickmund probes, thinking in balloons above his head. "I wonder if animals are plagued with the deeper questions of life? I wonder if they contemplate the mystery of eternal life?"

Faust, stares back. "I wonder if that's tuna or salmon I smell on his moustache?"

"I love it," I say, laughing out loud, picturing Faust twitching his nose to sneak a closer whiff of Sickmund's mustache.

"Thank you. Okay . . . now, in the television script, each episode will begin with Lenor drawn to her favorite comic strip, *Dr. Sickmund Fred*, in the morning paper. While she's reading, the characters come alive with animation. Though the other comics maintain their usual form, the Dr. Sickmund strip resembles a tiny movie screen projecting a cartoon world onto the printed page."

David stands up and paces. "Are you with me?"

I grin, nodding my head up and down with quick jerks.

"So, all of a sudden, Dr. Sickmund and Faust leap from the strip as cartoon characters and land in Lenor's world, transformed as life-sized animated puppets. They are therapist and client sharing their separate worlds in a magical way. Sickmund brings the cartoon world to Lenor and helps her see the lighter side of life. Through his humor and laid-back California therapy, Dr. Sickmund presents an 'animated' approach to a sometimes uptight and confusing world. It is this special mix of fantasy and realism that make sparks fly at Lenor's place."

David points down at the book. "In this one, Estelle is sitting at her desk when Sickmund yells, "Estelle! Why did you change my diagnosis of Mr. Rockwell? I can't even pronounce all these symptoms! Darn it all, he's one of our wealthiest clients!"

"And you dare to insult him with simple depression?" Estelle replies.

"That's hilarious," I say. "Go ahead, read me another one. I'm beginning to catch on to this zany Dr. Sickmund."

"Okay, the next episode focuses on the mystery of Lenor's connection to the cartoon world. She makes an appointment to see Dr. Zuccolotto, creator of *Dr. Sickmund Fred*, under the guise of therapy. She wants to discuss the strange experiences she's had while reading the comic strip. Dr. Z tries to convince her that daydreams about Dr. Sickmund are a harmless reaction to stress.

After Lenor finishes her session and departs, Dr. Z walks to his drawing board and looks at the cartoon he's been working on. Instantly, Dr. Sickmund comes alive before his eyes and says, "She's getting a little too close."

That very afternoon, I called Trey Scott, a long-time friend and local television producer.

"You'd better get over here, Trey. I've got to introduce you to David."

"Who the hell is David?"

"He's a guy I just met, and he's got this crazy, terrific idea for a television sitcom."

To make a long story short, Trey, David and I got together and wrote a television treatment. With dreams of Hollywood fame and fortune, we leaped into my beat-up, old Chrysler Le Baron and drove south. Pooling our meager resources, we rented a suite at the cheesy, old Park Hotel on Sunset Boulevard and set up headquarters. Considering our circumstances, I was delighted we could afford the accommodations, and that my two gentlemanly companions afforded me the pleasure of the larger of the two rooms, which they took to calling "The Lady's Suite." As for Trey and David, they made do with the small front room where they slept on the couch and floor.

On our first morning in Hollywood, David woke up in a state of nervous anxiety.

"Do you think we'll get to see any producers? And . . . will they like Sickmund? Huh? What do you guys think?"

"Take one of my Valiums," I suggested, as I reached for my purse. "It'll calm you down."

"Valium? Are you crazy! It's the most addictive drug known to man."

"What are you talking about? I've been taking it for twenty years and I'm not addicted."

David hit the wall, laughing.

Then came a tremendous pounding on the door.

Half-naked, struggling to put his pants on, Trey opened the door to a pretty embarrassing scene: clothes, blankets and pillows scattered everywhere, and me hollering from the Lady's Suite, "David, where's my leg? I gotta get dressed!"

It turned out to be Trey's dad, a portly, affable television producer.

"Sorry to wake you, kids," he said, "but we need to prepare you for your meetings."

Day after day, for two long weeks, we pitched our proposal

to directors, producers, and heads of studios at NBC, Hanna-Barbera and Paramount.

"We love ya, Baby, we'll be calling!"

But there were no calls.

Driving home to Santa Cruz, exhausted and disappointed, we rehashed the highs and lows of our Hollywood escapade and managed to laugh them off.

"Well, at least we met with top producers."

"Yeah, and it was good to practice pitching Sickmund."

"And our hotel wasn't toooo bad . . ."

And by some miracle, some magic of showbiz, we arrived back in Santa Cruz with the wondrous, irrepressible comic spirit which brought us all together in the first place.

Laughter and friendship, at any age is the best therapy.

Dr. Sickmund may seem a bit out of place in a book about aging. However, I included it because I wanted to show that it doesn't matter if you feel young and foolish, or old and foolish, just follow your dreams. The book that is in your hands, my third, was a dream at seventy-six years old. Dreams keep one involved and active. But, to keep them alive they need to be pursued.

Diana C.

When her dream became a possibility.

———

In 2004, I attended the college graduation of a friend's daughter. After the ceremony, I said to another friend, "I have always dreamed of getting my Ph.D."

"Great idea. You should do it," he said enthusiastically.

Encouraged, I held onto the dream until I talked to a fellow teacher who had just gotten his Ph.D. and told me how much it cost. At that, my dream faded. Nonetheless, I mentioned it a few years later to yet another friend, a college professor. He said, "What a splendid idea."

"Yes, but I can't afford it."

"Diana," he said, "get a GTF—a Graduate Teaching Fellowship—and it pays for it all."

I grabbed my dream. If I went to the University of Oregon, I thought, I could do the three-hour commute twice weekly and not have to close my mountain home. My supervisor at Rogue Community College, where I taught, said I could teach a four-hour class on Friday afternoons and keep my job there. A Ph.D. in English at UO would be a six-year commitment. I applied for a GTF and for the Ph.D. program. When I was accepted for both, the dream became possibility.

Moving to a city after forty years on the mountain, where I lived without electricity, was intimidating, but my friends were encouraging. As cities go, they said, Eugene was not very big.

I bought a bicycle. I rented a garage apartment, with a large garden in back. I bought an electric lamp, a toaster oven, and a cell phone. I got a map of Eugene and a map of the campus. I signed up for fall classes, packed the car, and headed for graduate school.

I loved it. Being on the beautiful UO campus was a constant pleasure. Teaching university students was a pleasure. Taking classes was a pleasure. Riding my bicycle through the park to campus was a pleasure. And going home for a four-day weekend was worth the long drive on the freeway.

But the dream had its nightmarish aspects. In a strange city and decades older than my classmates, I felt as though I existed only in the present, with an unknown past and an irrelevant future. My classmates were preparing for the lives ahead of them, whereas my life and my career, which nobody knew anything about, were mostly behind me. The first few years of graduate school were the most dissociative experiences of my life.

Things got better as I made friends. The real nightmare was the oral exams.

I walked into the examination room feeling ready, but when I sat down in front of my three interlocutors, professors I knew well, all my confidence fled and with it every thought I ever had about Old English and Medieval literature. My mind was empty. Every time I searched for the answer to a question, I felt like I was lowering a bucket into a well that contained no water. The bucket clanged against the rock sides and came up empty every time, except when it brought up a frog or a snake, answers so wrong they were ugly. Dr. Jim Earl, my advisor, looked like he wanted to crawl through the floor. Dr. Anne Laskaya kept asking me easier and easier questions, none of which I could answer. Dr. Martha Bayless just looked incredulous. I was a complete dunce. It was everything I could do to keep from crying. It was by far the most humiliating experience of my life.

When it was over, I was told to sit in the foyer while the committee decided whether I had passed. I waited a long, long time. Finally, Jim called me back into the room. They told me I had passed. I could continue with the program. I could move on to writing my dissertation.

Of course, in reality I had failed the exam, but they passed me anyway because, after all, I wasn't headed towards a university career, and, as Jim kept asking Martha Bayless, "What do you do about a good student with a bad exam?" I don't know what

Martha's arguments were, but in the end Jim and Anne convinced her to let me pass.

My dream had almost crumbled, but from that point on, it blossomed. I wrote my dissertation, on Old English secular poetry, as a series of short essays. I thoroughly enjoyed that writing—the scholarship, the ideas, the crafting of words and thoughts.

Remembering the disaster of the oral exams, I was nervous about the defense of my dissertation, the last step before being able to receive a Ph.D. at graduation. It would be the same sort of thing: three professors asking me questions, except this time it would be public. Anyone could come. I had friends drive up from the Applegate. Another friend drove in from central Oregon. My landlady came.

Colleagues came. Except for my nervousness, the atmosphere was slightly charged with excitement, but also casual and almost fun. The three professors turned the whole thing into a chat with me, but I was so nervous I was on the verge of tears. I could feel Anne Laskaya, one of the professors on my defense committee, boring her eyes into me: Look at me. Look at me. When I finally worked up nerve to look at her, she gave me a big wink!

When it was over, Jim, my advisor, asked me and all the guests to step outside while the committee determined whether or not I had passed. As soon as I left the room, I broke into a gush of tears. My friends *surrounded me. They said I had done a great job. They said they never could have answered such difficult questions. I was cocooned in their love and comfort and support while we waited to know the outcome.*

Jim stepped out of the room into the corridor. We all looked at him. He said, "Is Doctor Coogle here?"

Cathy

A house in paradise?

Sometime after my divorce, I started a little export clothing business that brought me to Mexico once a month. My little business took off and I had so much fun developing it and working at it. It made me feel optimistic and hopeful.

The trips to Mexico were a great distraction from the daily routine. The people there are so fun loving and hospitable. I love the food, the climate and the attitude of the people. I decided then and there that I was going to have a house in Puerto Vallarta when I retired and live there six months out of the year. Was I crazy or what!! I did not have a pot to piss in as they say. What was I thinking? A house here in paradise?

After some health scares and financial difficulties, I sold four of my clothing franchises which paid my mortgage and my late bills. Next, I became a happy and successful real-estate agent.

After fourteen years and my initial goal regarding Mexico, I started a search for my place in the sun. I eventually bought a house in Cabo San Lucas, Mexico, on a mountain, with a panoramic ocean view where I now live four months out of the year.

Sharon B.

"I have fulfilled my mission."

———

I have recently retired after thirty years of directing theater in my community. Bittersweet and nostalgic, I have come to the end of my career here. Not without many accolades and many of my students doing amazing things like Broadway debuts and touring shows. I have had so many memories onstage and off that I can honestly say I have fulfilled my mission of bringing live theater to my community. It has been a joyous life and I will continue to spread the joy of live theater wherever I land.

Fortunately, that has brought me to the next chapter, bringing my production company to the jungle of Costa Rica and so the journey continues!

Susan

"I want to be a Master Gardener one day!"

———

Years ago, I had a neighbor who was a phenomenal gardener who had an extraordinarily beautiful garden. I had just purchased a little house across the street from her that had a perfectly dismal yard. She was patient and generous with her advice whenever I had a question about where to plant a shrub or how to prune the perennials.

One day, I asked her how she happened to come by so much gardening expertise. She told me she had become a Master Gardener through the University Extension program and I decided then and there that I wanted to do that someday.

Years later, after I had retired, I took the course, met a hundred other kindred gardening geeks, and became a certified Master Gardener. It's been one of my proudest accomplishments.

Diane H.

"I took a gamble."

———

My first marriage was to a city-man, an avid sailor. Despite my childhood dream of marrying a cowboy like my sister and living on a horse ranch, we bought a house in the bucolic suburbia of Marin County. We were married for eleven years and had two wonderful daughters. Yet, I found my relationship with my husband similar to my mother's relationship with my philandering father. At the age of thirty-six, I made the choice to break the cycle.

I got a divorce and went back to college to finish my degree in business. After graduating, I went to work at a computer peripheral company, and after four years, I took a gamble, and opened my own computer peripheral company. It was a success . . . and I soon had it all! All that is . . . except the ranch. As a distributor, I figured I could live anywhere! So like Noah with his ark, I packed my SUV and horse trailer with two girls, two dogs, two cats, two horses, two birds, and two fish, left Marin County and headed for the foothills of the Sierras to pursue my childhood dream of owning a ranch. That dream was achieved at age forty-two!

I'm still here on the ranch. Most importantly, in keeping with my entrepreneurial spirit, I have turned my beloved horse ranch into the perfect Air B and B/ Horse Motel.

In the early mornings after feeding, kicking horse shit, and fixing fences, I sit on a big granite rock and survey all that I dreamed of as a five-year-old child and say to myself, "You Did Good Girl!"

Not me, or anyone else I knew would have imagined that I would one day become an author. It was a pretty big dream at the time. We women of a certain age know the secret of chasing dreams. What is it? It's about giving ourselves permission to pursue whatever lights us up. It's wonderful to accomplish a longed-for dream. But the real secret is chasing them. You'll never feel more alive.

Chapter Thirteen

Dreaded Menopause

"I call the Change of Life 'Orchids' because menopause is such an ugly word. It's got men in it for God's sake."

~ Lisa Jey Davis

Hot flashes? Weight gain? Memory problems?

I've known women who sailed through "the change" with hardly a blip and I've known others who suffered and wailed like screaming banshees. I, fortunately, did not have a hard experience. In fact, my daughters have asked me, "how come you never went through menopause, Mom?"

"I did, my darlings, I just never talked about it."

Perhaps, because my mother complained about it all the time and for a very long time, I being young, and not understanding, was not very sympathetic. So, when my time came, I never wanted my daughters or anyone else for that matter, to listen to me sound off on the grimness of menopause.

This worked for me, even when "hot flashes" invaded my space with sweats, chills and irritability, I did my best to ignore the symptoms and brush them off with a glib, "Oh, my what a hot day it is."

Here's how some of the ladies coped.

Cynthia

I was fifty when I experienced the lovely state of hot flashes, usually during a conference or a new business presentation of course. They only lasted a few months and my transition was relatively painless. The age thing had never bothered me at all, until I realized I had entered the fifty-to-sixty-five age bracket on surveys. That was quite a shock! I certainly didn't think like a sixty-five-year-old person! How could I be grouped with them? Now, I'm seventy-one and just accept/ignore the crisscross of wrinkles and sagging neck and blotchy skin. Time for others to shine!

L.A.

"I worked out my own plan."

———

Menopause . . . not fun! Need I say more? I made the choice to use Hormone Replacement Therapy because I could not deal with the way menopause affected my well-being. As a young child, I remember my mother (who had me late in life) screaming for years, "I'm going through the Change!"

She would send me outside to play in the heat of the summer as she took her three-hour naps. I would agonize over sneaking back into the house for a cool drink, meaning I had to carefully open the old, screen door that stuck and then would slam shut causing a loud bang. I knew there would be hell to pay. It wasn't until I was going through my own 'change' that I could empathize with her.

Now it was my turn, and after several tries my doctor got me on a program that worked, sorta. I would take Estrogen for so many days and end the month with Progesterone. I was fine during the Estrogen phase but the Progesterone caused me great discomfort. My doctor agreed to have me take the Progesterone every three months and have a biopsy test taken every six months. Well, Progesterone time equaled "Hell time." So, I worked out my own plan, taking Estrogen all the time (life was good) and Progesterone (Hell time), once in a blue moon.

I went along with my plan for several years, then, after about my third biopsy, cancer reared its ugly head. The doctor suggested a complete hysterectomy "We will have to go through your abdomen to determine if it has spread to other areas." She was stern as she delivered the news. I knew she probably could get the job done but I also knew vanity was not her priority. I must find another plan.

At that time, I had a Brazilian friend who was a hairdresser. She told me about these amazing Brazilian doctors, a gynecologist and two plastic surgeons, that worked in tandem. They were excellent and charged a fraction of the cost. I was amazed as she bared her beautiful flat stomach with pride. She did a hysterectomy and a tummy tuck at the same time. Brilliant! I knew this was something my American doctor knew nothing about.

My friend had started an extra business to accompany friends and clients to Brazil and help them get checked into the clinic. So off to Brazil I went.

Once in San Pablo, I met with the gynecologist and the famous plastic surgeons. The doctor would perform the hysterectomy and then the plastic surgeons would perform the tummy tuck. My kind of plan! It had vanity written all over it . . . now this appealed to me! My friend had to translate as no one there spoke English, but even so, I felt confident that I was going to be well taken care of.

The surgery went well. The doctors were certain they got every bit of cancer as their tests later confirmed. Although I was in pain and swollen, everything was a great success.

The next thing I knew I woke up in a small room with a bathroom. These two very sweet nurses were sitting by my side. They kept saying "Beautiful, so beautiful," as they stroked my platinum blonde hair.

For $25 a day, I decided to splurge and stay at the clinic for three more days. I had my nurses all to myself and the doctors made their morning stops. We made do with sign language the best we could. When I had to go to the bathroom, I would make a pussssh sound, we'd laugh and they'd escort me to the bathroom.

All good things come to an end, however, and it was time to leave the gilded Clinico and go stay at the iron barred, chain linked, dog barking, babies crying, soup and sausage home of my friend's mom there in San Pablo. I had no choice. I was too weak to be on my own and was advised to walk bent over for two weeks, so as not to stretch my delicate tummy tuck stitches.

My recuperating room was about 8'x8' with a twin bed, a small window and an old TV. The mattress did *not have memory foam, of this I am certain. I was so uncomfortable I thought I was going to die! I was in too much pain to sleep. I just remember staring at the TV for hours and listening to the damn dogs bark.*

My friend's mom turned out to be an un-nurturing bitch. Thank God their eldest son had learned English. He became my friend. We would hang out on the back porch and watch the monkeys steal the fruit off the trees. He showed me how to use his email so I could communicate with my children and friends at home. A call from my kids was like a call from Heaven. I knew I could make it but couldn't wait to get back home.

Once home, I had a chance to reflect on what I had done and the choices I had made. It could have been a complete disaster. Even though I didn't have the support of most of my friends (who flat out said I was crazy to do this), I was very happy I took that chance. In the end, I had a great result and an experience that I will never forget.

Susan

"A surge in creativity and energy."

———

I think it was Margaret Mead that said once you were through with menopause you would have a surge of energy and creativity like never before. I'm still waiting for that. All I can say is she'd better be right! I had a hysterectomy at forty. They left me one ovary but I still needed some help so I tried Hormone Replacement Therapy. It was hard to tell if it really helped. HRT exacerbated my lupus symptoms so much, I decided to stop taking it. I still have occasional hot flashes but if I avoid certain trigger foods, they don't seem too bad.

Yes, I get the brain fog. Yes, I got the weight gain. But on the whole, I'm fine. And actually, I think I have seen a little surge in creativity and energy. That could be menopause, or it could just be that I'm older, wiser and happier now.

Diana

"Forget it all. Who cares now?"

———

I saw a friend recently at a party, a man I hadn't seen for a long time. We had a long, wonderful conversation, but there was something he said that I didn't have a chance to answer at the time. At one point in our conversation, just before he was called to the other room to play music, he said, "Do women have a mid-life crisis, too?"

Do women have a mid-life crisis, Walter? Just listen to what Nature tells a woman in her fifties:

"So you're not going to produce any more children?" Nature says with a sneer. "Well, you're not worth much, then. Procreation is everything. All those things I gave you to make the opposite sex lust after you? Forget them. You don't need them anymore. That nice high lift to the breasts? Let them fall. That blush on the cheek, that taut skin, those full red lips, that waspish figure? Forget it all. Who cares now? Let the face wash out and the lip line recede. Let the waist thicken and the thighs sag and the shapely hips go slack. Let the flesh hang, let the skin wrinkle. Who cares now? Go ahead; be an elephant. Those lovely tresses with their sheen and shine? No need; let them thin out, lose their color, turn brittle. Those healthy, strong bones? Let 'em break, if they're going to. You're of no more use to me, so I toss you aside. Rot, go to ruin, try to recover my gifts with lipstick, bras, and hair dye. Do what you like. You don't interest me anymore."

But indifference isn't enough for Nature. She also turns vindictive. "The curse" is not a woman's period but the cessation of that period. Listen to Nature's curse, Walter:

"May you wake up night after night in a sudden heat, sweating furiously," Nature begins. "May you throw off the covers and splay out your limbs, only

to shiver minutes later with a sudden chill. May your nights alternate between being dream-drenched and sweat-drenched, and may your days be plagued with internal combustion. At any time during the day, may these waves of fire wash over your body. May your face blush red and shine with sweat and then grow mottled as a molting parrot, and may these things occur three or four times an hour, in the most embarrassing of all social and professional circumstances when you can't walk outside to cooler air or fan yourself frantically or gulp cold water. May there also be a social stigma on this condition of your age so you can't say, 'Whew! Hot flash!' but can only pretend like nothing is happening or that no one will notice. May the heat be so intense that everyone notices, and may it come on you desperately hot during a romantic dinner or while teaching class or playing tennis or having a guitar lesson. And on top of all that, may you one minute revel in euphoria and the next want to bite off the heads of your friends and snap at your cats, and may you be forced to admit that if the bitchiness is unreasonable, so is the euphoria. And so may it be for you on the threshold between youth and old age."

Do women have a mid-life crisis, too? Tell me, Walter, what on earth is a man's mid-life crisis like?

As you can see, we gals have all experienced menopause uniquely. But however we went through, got through, or breezed through it, we have noted it as a milestone, because it is. If we were in a more tribal culture, we'd now be recognized as Wise Women, respected and revered for our advice and experience. Women of a certain age clearly have a role to play. Maybe that's what menopause really is, a portal to a phase of our lives where we come to realize our own true value.

Chapter Fourteen

Faith

"Faith is taking the first step even when you don't see the whole staircase."

~ Martin Luther King, Jr.

My faith is a foundational belief that there is something greater than myself, something I can call on that guides me, loves me, hears me and gives me motivation and the ability to keep going despite life's demands.

When I was diagnosed with cancer and told I would require an amputation to survive, I could do nothing but hand it over to the universe and pray. And just to be sure I had God's ear, I plea bargained on the night before surgery: "If you cure me of this cancer, I promise I will do anything, feed the poor, visit the sick, anything if you grant me one wish . . . my life. It was my *"promessa."*

The universe worked its magic. I lived through the operation and was cured of cancer. It was then that I wondered, how I might fulfill my *promessa?* I knew it was something I had to do as I couldn't take a chance that God might back out of our bargain.

During the ensuing years, the *promessa* was always on my mind, and it led me down different, unimaginable paths. As I gained strength and adjusted to my new-found circumstance, people encouraged me to write my story. Maybe, I thought, this was one way I could help satisfy my *promessa* by offering hope and inspiration to others in desperate situations. So, I put my faith in God and prayed to write a worthy book that could help change lives.

After the publication and success of *One Step at a Time,* I was suddenly in demand to speak at churches, universities, to patients in hospital beds, private homes, television, radio and in the press to tell my story. Thankfully, I loved doing it and I know as a fact that my *promessa* has changed lives.

I remember back when I was invited to all the major religious TV shows to share my story, including *Praise the Lord* with Jim and Tammy Baker.

The PTL Club had millions of viewers and checks arrived daily. I didn't like the show or believe in its message, but I thought it would be one more way to fulfill my *promessa*—not to mention, sell a few books.

I arrived at Charleston South Carolina's International Airport. A shiny Rolls Royce, picked me up, compliments of the Bakers. Luxuriating in the back seat, I could hear Jimmy Baker blaring from the television set, "You send me your last social security check and I promise, heavens gates will open to you."

"God, Lenor, are you sure you want to be a part of this show?" I asked myself.

I rationalized that my appearance was not about cheating folks out of their money, but about my *promessa* and the hopes of making a difference in people's lives.

The morning of the show, I sat with Tammy on the set with a huge audience in attendance.

Tammy was crying before even asking me the question: "How did you lose your leg?" When I answered, fresh tears with prodigious amounts of black mascara trailed down her cheeks.

"No, no, this is not a sad story, Tammy, it's a heartwarming story. I even have a beautiful, artificial leg that I'm wearing," I looked out to the audience. "Would you like to see it?"

The audience stood up and cheered. Tammy continued with the flow of tears.

"Well, ladies and gentlemen, I'm not going to drop my pants" laughter erupting from the audience, "but, I will pull up my pant leg, so you can see it."

One Step at a Time hit the Religious Best Seller list, and I didn't have to drop my pants. Praise the Lord!

Sharon C.

———

Wisdom does come with age and I feel we navigate life in a more sensible way due to our experience. Not to say we don't mess up as we are still learning the lessons as life is ever changing.

For me personally, this is where God enters the picture. The power of prayer and positive thinking will always carry us through whatever challenges we must face. Thanks to my deep faith in God, I feel healthy and content about myself most days. I also believe God has a plan for all of us, which is our fate.

J.J.

"Divine Guidance is for my highest good."

———

As I understand it, we create our own reality. It is in knowing our thoughts, attitudes, beliefs and feelings are the intentions we set forth that activate the power needed to manifest our desires.

I decided a long time ago not to 'believe' anything because there is always more to become aware of and understand. I embrace the on-going information that somehow finds its way to me or falls in my path.

That is what I consider Divine Guidance, and it is for my highest good. It is my heart's desire to embody unconditional love. I understand God to be the divine intelligent creator which we are all a spark of. We have the opportunity to become aware of our oneness, that we are all connected within this oneness through all the cosmos.

I am really set on the intention of meditation every day. It's kinda the place to visit and hang out, breathing into our lungs and beating our hearts, because it is eternal. The more we do it, the more it makes us eternally youthful, vibrantly healthy, radiantly beautiful and opulently abundant in the proportion of our sincere belief and trust in that possibility.

L.A.

"We pretty much choose our destiny."

———

I married young and had two children from my first marriage which lasted ten years. Being out on my own for the first time in my life gave me a huge opportunity to grow. I dove head-first into self-help books, went to EST, discovered my inner-child, and meditated, but I credit my faith-based upbringing to always return me to what I believed was right. I have never strayed too far from my roots.

I believe we pretty much choose our destiny. Whatever we choose or cause, we will have to accept the effect. If we obey the rules of the road, in other words, the traffic laws, (obeying the speed limit, stopping at the stop lights, yielding, no texting while driving, etc.) we will be less likely to get injured, ticketed or even killed . . . Same goes for obeying the Ten Commandments. If you follow God's Law your chances of living a happier, safer and longer life are much higher.

Cathy

———

Praying is a tool that I use every day. Supplication! The action of asking or begging for something passionately, heartfelt or humbly. I asked this of God. Please Lord help me through this.

Susan

"I create my own church."

———

I sometimes describe myself as a Buddhist-Christian-Pagan. Having a connection to a 'Higher Power' is very central to who I am. From my upbringing in a Christian household, I have a strong underpinning of daily prayer. From the Buddhist tradition I find the practice of mindfulness and meditation to be grounding.

And from my "woo-woo" more pagan beliefs, I am sure that God speaks to me all the time through whatever I am most open to, which for me is most often in Nature.

When I lived off-grid up in the mountains, I once spent months making a labyrinth of stones that I would visit almost daily and do some silent walking meditation around the circle there. It became a very sacred place for me, because I invested so much spiritual energy there. Building that circle of stones was like creating my own church. Walking that labyrinth helped me when my mind was unsettled, or my emotions were scattered.

The word that sums up my faith has to be 'gratitude.' Being grateful helps me to appreciate more of the beauty around us. I recognize the little things more than I did when I was younger. I can geek out now over bird nests, and pebbles and the bark of trees.

This whole world is such a miracle and a wonder. I believe that the sacred resides in gratitude for everything from the mundane to the magnificent, and even the heart-breaking. We can't pick out just the things we love and enjoy and call them holy. Every moment, every person, bird, tree, mountain, friend and neighbor are part of this grand creation and worthy of our love.

Cynthia

I was brought up Catholic but don't go to church. (Two particular priests angered me, and I haven't gotten over it.) But I am a believer. A book by Richard Bach, Illusions: Confessions of a Reluctant Messiah, is my bible. I believe in myself, in luck, and in thanking whoever is responsible for me for helping me through tough times and for helping my kids when I can't. I believe in rainbows and lucky pennies and have almost always had the best luck in the world!

Diana C.

"I'm always counting my blessings!"

———

Last week I received a poem from a poet friend, suggesting that everyone should have a secret place, a place to be alone for renewal, reflection, and recharge, for counting one's blessings, he says, instead of curses. He suggests some possibilities: "a hidden waterfall, a garden corner, a favorite walk, a mini shrine in a bedroom. "It's personal," he says, "not advertised, no chorus girls, no signage," and he suggests that it might include "a photograph or a seashell from that day, a broken toy, a lock of hair."

I like his poem, but reading it makes me anxious. As a person who likes to think of herself as the sort of person the poem suggests, I must, therefore, have a secret and sacred place, but where is it? Is it my writing nook, where I sit at my computer, alternately gazing at the mountain and putting thoughts on paper? That is a way of reflecting and recharging, but the writing nook is also, by definition, a workspace, which, by definition, doesn't sound sacred.

Maybe my sacred space is the couch, where I sit to gaze on the mountain and reflect while I knit and where I renew my intellect with the New Yorker or the *latest book I'm reading.*

But there doesn't seem to be anything sacred or secret about a couch against a wall in an open room, and if I am sometimes contemplative while I knit there, at other times I'm learning the hard lessons of patience as I undo my mistakes. There is no photograph near the couch; all my seashells are in the bathroom, and the rocks, bones, and pieces of wood I've gathered over the years sit on windowsills and shelves throughout the house, so there is no meditative focus, except that I do keep a coffee-table book of flower photographs at the side of the couch, turning a page once a day, so that, as I walk by the table, I stop for a moment to admire the photograph that has caught my eye. That's hardly a meditation, just a quick moment of admiration.

Because the couch lacks privacy, it seems more reasonable to think my sacred space is my bed. Sleep is renewal, and when I awake every morning and gaze at the mountain, I am always, always counting my blessings, though it seems a cheat to call the bed a sacred space, since I'm there by necessity, sort of like saying my sacred space is the bathtub. We go to bed to sleep and we bathe to get clean, although rest and renewal and also reflection come with those activities, at least for me.

The fainting couch in the library might seem like a secret place, except that I don't use it that way. I don't go there deliberately to renew but only when I need a book from the library or wander into the library just to enjoy looking at my books. This place only looks like a meditative spot. It doesn't function that way, sort of the way the bed looks like a functional space but functions like a meditative space.

I do have a favorite walk—up the mountain. I also know of a secret waterfall I can access from my house, but it's hard to get to. Although I certainly consider it sacred (all nature is sacred), I don't go there very often. Either choice, life, like the bed and the bathtub, is functional, really (for the exercise), with the side effect of meditation.

So where is my sacred place? If I am that sort of person, I must have one.

I do. It is big and spacious, not the sort of exclusive place indicated by the poem, but, still, my place of meditation, renewal, reflection. It is my home, inside and out, here on the mountain—all the places I mentioned above, its zen garden with canvas-back chairs, its deck with its flower boxes, its garden with take-a-rest chairs, and, from everywhere, its view of the mountain. It is not advertised, and there are no chorus girls, but its signage speaks truth. "Wonderland:" where wonder fills the psyche and gratitude spreads bright wings.

Love and faith and gratitude seem to be the rocks that we women of a certain age stand on. Faith has a role to play in both our joys and our sorrows. Knowing that there is more to this life than what we can see has brought us to the realization that we ourselves might be the eyes and ears and hands of God.

Chapter Fifteen

Shape of Our Days

*"One day your life will flash before your eyes.
Make sure it's worth watching."*

~ Gerard Way

I thought it might be interesting for readers to get a feeling of what normal days are like for some women of a certain age. After all, the quality of our lives is made up of all the thousand little things we spend our time doing, like eating, sleeping, working, playing. Things that seem mundane might be the things we end up valuing most—a pleasant meal, a quiet day with our husband, a beautiful sunset.

The first thing I do when I wake up in the morning and

step out of bed is thank God for all my blessings! It's essential. Then, I join Roix in the living room to enjoy morning coffee together while reading and discussing the morning newspapers or local and national television news shows. I like to call my girls as often as possible and return or make calls to friends. After breakfast, I go to my office to write.

Roix, usually has a million and one things to keep occupied. Lately, he's revisiting riding and maintaining motorcycles; or, because he's known in the neighborhood as the "fix-it" man, he's called on almost daily to fix a washing machine, hang curtains or level someone's driveway with his tractor. "Lenor, may I borrow your husband today?" is a familiar call.

In the summer, I try to finish work by four p.m. to get to the pool for exercise.

My brother, Ernie, called recently saying how lucky we were to have a pool and waterfall surrounded by manicured lawns. I think Ernie misunderstood my description of the pool. In actuality, the 'pool' is a rubber, above-ground pool about four feet deep, the 'waterfall' is a PVC pipe that Roix rigged up to a filter pump and the 'manicured lawn' is in the middle of a pasture. So much for Lenor's notable exaggerations!

Roix and I enjoy wine in the evenings, a nice dinner, then we watch TV and hit the sack to read. A simple day and evening with my husband shapes most of my days. However, when we're on the road in our pick-up truck with bikes in tow, searching for new bike trails, or in the air flying cross country in our small plane, or traveling to Mexico or Costa Rica for holidays, our days, of course, take on different schedules—meeting people; discovering new places; and experiencing the joy of not knowing what the day will bring.

We usually don't make reservations. Back to when I first met Roix, and before going on my first flying trip with him, I asked if we should make reservations?

"No reservations for me. I just get in the plane, slam the door and take off!"

"I'm with you, Baby!" I laughed.

It's such a privilege to be able to form one's days. Of course, when you're working eight to five, a part of your day is already defined, but most of our time is in our own hands and we can do what we choose. For me, it's either furiously writing to make a deadline or cuddled up on the couch with a warm blanket, my cat, Cruiser, and reading a book—and I never feel guilty that I'm not doing more . . .

Susan

"My days are a little more sedentary
than is healthy."

I love lazy mornings these days. I used to schedule everything before noon, it was always zoom zoom hurry hurry. Nowadays I won't go anywhere or even answer the phone before eleven a.m.

I'm still an early riser though. I like the feeling

of possibilities that mornings offer. When I get up, I head straight for the coffee pot, then a shower, have a leisurely breakfast, watch the news, read the paper, spend time on the internet, walk the dog, do a bit of yoga and meditation. By then, it can be noon if I'm being really being pokey!

In the middle part of my day, I work on whatever projects are on the schedule; writing, sewing, yard work, errands, housework, etc.

I usually have an early dinner and watch TV in the evenings. I generally have a glass of wine or a cocktail or smoke a little cannabis in the evenings, but not always. Sometimes I just have tea.

I think my average day is probably more sedentary than is healthy and that is something I need to change. I do get out and walk the dog twice a day along the river, but it's a pretty short walk. I'm outside in the garden nearly every day in the spring and summer, but in winter and fall, I'm in slow-motion.

My social life is pretty low key. I love my friends but I don't seem to need to spend much time hanging out in the same ways I used to.

Life is pretty quiet and I like it that way for the most part. Being alone has it's perks. I've spent most of my life doing for others. Nowadays it's a soothing balm to have my days to myself.

I knew a ninety-two-year-old woman who told me years ago "time alone is very consoling." I didn't *really get it then, but I do now. Whenever I spend time socially with people, even people I know and love, I can hardly wait to get home, take my fucking bra off and put my feet up!*

Cynthia

Cynthia likes the fact that simple living involves less cleaning.

Daily life as a full time "RVer" in our 17' travel trailer, Yacht Enough: Up around eight a.m., when I smell the Starbucks brewing in the French Press.

Camouflage our standard-sized bed into a lounge via a cream-colored, sheep-skin blanket, three huge, contrasting throw pillows and several stuffed ocean inhabitants to keep me feeling as close to the sea as possible (an octopus, whale shark, blue tang, parrot fish, spotted eagle, sting ray and of course a pelican).

Whip out the hand vac to clear our two-foot by six-foot floor and a small floor mat. The beauty of our simple living is little to no cleaning!

Outside to sit in the lounge chair or rocker and plan our activities, if any. . . . (Every day is Saturday when you're retired so schedules are rarely obstacles.)

Maybe it's to the pool, or to visit fellow travelers,

*or working on our book sales or reading or talking
with grandchildren.*

Diana

"The days were turning into an amorphous blob."

———

*For years, my days were shaped by the academic
calendar. When the teaching came to an abrupt end,
suddenly my days lacked any shape at all. I missed
teaching. I missed being around young people and
learning what they think. I missed the classroom and
the challenge of teaching students how to write with
graceful prose, how to apply critical thinking, how to
recognize creditable sources. Teaching was my tiny
contribution towards a better world. Even though I
only taught two days a week, my days were shaped by
grading papers, preparing syllabi, and brainstorming
lessons in addition to the time in the classroom.*

*I never worried about the shape of my days after
I retired because, after all, I had been a part-time
writer as well as a part-time teacher, a career that
left me time to do other things, too: reading, sewing,
hiking, backpacking, cross-country skiing. But then, I
was forced to retire. Suddenly my days were shapeless.
It wasn't so much that I didn't know what to do with*

my time as that I felt my usefulness in life had been snatched out from under me. The days were turning into an amorphous blob.

Gradually I learned how to give shape to my days, mostly by creating challenges for myself. How hard could I hike? Could I do seventy-five things of seventy-five repetitions each in one year?

Then Mike stepped into my life, and I began to shape my days around him. When we decided to get married, we agreed we would not live together day after day and night after night (after all these years— not a good idea). Nonetheless, my days were shaped by this relationship. And I loved their shape.

We can order our lives only to a certain extent. A year after our wedding, my husband died. I came home to my own house to learn how to reshape my days, this time around grief. I felt the way I had, after I returned home after earning my Ph.D. in 2012: "Before enlightenment, chopping wood and carrying water. After enlightenment, chopping wood and carrying water," as in this Golden Shovel poem I wrote (meaning that the Zen saying is laid out in the last word of each line):

Living Zen

I went and got my Ph.D. before
I was seventy, and then with that intellectual
enlightenment
I came home again and found myself
chopping
Vegetables for dinner and hauling wood
For the fire to warm the house and
Wondered what difference it made,
all that hauling
Of books and stimulating the mind with
ancient water.
Then I got married, after
I was seventy, and lived the enlightenment
Of love until cancer came chopping
Down my beloved liked a piece of wood
For the funeral pyre and
Left me hauling
My emptiness around like a bucket of water.

The emptiness comes to us from time to time, un-shaping our days and forcing us to create ourselves anew. When it does, whether from retirement or a death or a pandemic that locks us in our houses, we have to create, again, the meaningfulness of our lives. Today, I shape my life around the family that the corona virus temporarily prevents me from visiting, the writing that has always been my mainstay, crafts that I enjoy, and, most of all, hiking day after day, by myself or with a friend, in these beautiful mountains I have called home for half a century.

It's clear that women of a certain age value the freedom that retirement brings. We like being able to structure our days according to our tastes, interests and whims. We value our time and want to make the most of it. If we choose to work, we focus on doing work that we love, work than inspires. If we choose to play, we like to engage in activities that enliven and inspire us.

Working or playing, we want to enjoy our time, not simply mark our time.

Chapter Sixteen

What I Know Now

"Imagination is everything. It is the preview of life's coming attractions."

~ Albert Einstein

The years have passed all too quickly since my seventieth birthday. Back then, I expressed a fear of growing old and I needed to ignite my desire to avoid thinking about age. Now, with eighty looming, I ask myself, have I been able to create an energetic, positive, outlook on this uncharted byway of aging?

Yes, I have. What has sustained me through the years is maintaining good health, work, travel, family and friends. I am living my legacy in real time rather than having the preacher talk about it at my funeral. I learn from the past; live in the present, and build for the future.

What I know now, but did not know after my amputation, was how challenging it would be to sustain good physical health. Over the years, my hands and one knee have suffered, not only by overuse, but also by me not accepting help or assistance when needed.

As an example: In the past, when traveling alone on an airplane, too ashamed to ask for a wheelchair, I struggled to get to the gates, sometimes even missing flights.

Now, I always have a wheelchair waiting for me.

"Shall I push you to the handicap section to wait for your next plane?" the attendant will ask over my shoulder.

"No, thank you, just take me to the bar."

He offers a smile and pushes me directly to the bar where I hop off the chair, onto the bar stool and place my foot on the chair making sure it isn't absconded.

"Thank you very much, be back in thirty minutes," I wink.

"You got it, Miss," he says, still smiling.

Stubbornness, in not asking for help when needed, ultimately led to my knee and thumbs giving out. I was scared to death. Oh, no, what will I do now?

To my relief, my doctor said I had options.

Grateful, to be given choices, I've had successful surgery on my right shoulder, both hands and a total knee replacement— all within the last five years.

Options, how I love them. Even back when I was given the choice of amputation or keeping my leg and being treated with massive doses of chemotherapy and radiation, I chose surgery, and it saved my life.

What I feel now, is gratitude for being able to work at something I love. For me, writing takes time, effort and patience. But it gives me good reason to rise happily in the morning. To think, to remember, to imagine, and put it down on paper, is an awesome privilege.

Along with writing books, I enjoy writing for magazines.

When my grandkids were younger, they liked to sit on my lap while I was at my computer immersed in trying to write something inspirational for a magazine.

One afternoon, while I was composing an article on Coping with Cancer, my little five-year-old grandson was sitting on my lap with his chubby legs dangling off the seat of the chair.

"Let's see now," I said to myself, rubbing my chin, "losing my leg to cancer" (trying to think of something inspiring to write). "Losing my leg . . . ," hmm . . .

"Is a disaster!" Elliott shouted, looking up at me, his yellow curls bouncing across his forehead.

One may find it surprising, but recently I almost gave up on work. It happened when the publisher of this book accepted my proposal but I chose to decline. So, what was my problem?

After the initial joy of being accepted by a publisher, I started to think about all the work involved: re-writes; editing; promoting; advertising; marketing . . . and I wavered. "Will I be able to keep up with all that's involved with the publication of a third book at my age?"

I responded to my publisher that I was not going to sign

using the pandemic as my defense.

When I went to bed that night, before turning off the light, I said to my husband, "I feel like such a loser, not signing."

And my excuses didn't sit well with him or my publisher.

"It's up to you," Roix said, "but what about all your talk of living your legacy?"

"The pandemic should be under control by the time the book is released," my publisher said, trying to encourage me, "but I will not pressure you."

I reconsidered and once I'd signed, I was on a roll again—working and living high.

Travel is right at the top of my list of priorities, even at this age. How could it not be when my wanderlust husband, who snubs aging, will always ask when traveling: "I wonder where that road goes?"

Be it a dirt road in Central America, a bike path in Oregon or, up in his plane: "How would you like to fly to the Sierras and land on some of the airstrips where we've never landed before?"

"Oookay . . ."

From my early escapade hitch-hiking through Europe, to my first date with Roix flying in his 1946 Super Cruiser—all journeys have led to an obsessive need to keep on movin'.

Family and fun activities are essential to my well-being. Since my surgery, over forty-eight years ago, I have tried my best to do the things I used to do. Swimming (and not in circles), boating, flying, riding my ATV and electric trike, these are a few of the physical activities that could have been off limits for me if I'd not made the effort, and if I'd listened to some doctors who said, "You, must accept that you'll probably be in a wheelchair for the rest of your life." Wrong!!!

What is more important in life than family and friends? Nothing. To nourish these relationships with contact, love, communication, and interest in each of their lives, gives me the greatest of pleasure and garners respect both from and to them.

Because I've learned to embrace challenges, I have grown and become more of who I was meant to be—valued and vital. I'm living life much as I did when I was younger, perhaps a little more slowly.

However, my grandchildren may disagree with the 'slower' description. One of my favorite stories that sheds light on why my three grandchildren, Allie, Summer and Elliott, think otherwise . . .

One Christmas, to their delight, I invited them all to go for a ride with me on my ATV around the property. Before they hopped on, Allie, distracted by the warning printed on the fender, yelled out, "Grandma! It says here, 'Do not ride without a helmet, No more than one person and No alcohol!'

"No problem, my darlings, hop on—one in front, two in back and please do not topple my wine bottle tucked under the bungee cord."

What I know now, is that different voices rise as we age and, of course, the body is only one of the physical changes that takes place. It's one we are most aware of, perhaps, because we compare it to what we were, and how the world sees and values us as we age. My contributors and I, vibrantly agree that we have become the absolute best version of ourselves as we age.

A quote from a remarkable book, The Rainbow Comes and Goes, by Gloria Vanderbilt and her son Anderson Cooper, vividly describes the sentiment I live by and is close to my heart.

"Ever upward, as a new life, a new day begins. Have faith that something unexpected and wonderful is moving toward you at incredible speed."

EXCELSIOR!!!

Here are some thoughts from the ladies on *what they know now* . . .

Sharon B.

"We are all put on this earth for a purpose."

———

If someone would have said I'd live to be sixty-eight, I'd say you're crazy! I'm a little wider, wiser, and weathered but overall happy and healthy!

My relationships past and present have all molded me into the person I am today. Loves lost and gained. I have cherished raising my two daughters into the incredible women they are today. All one can hope is that your children achieve their goals and are have their own loves.

It's funny to hear people say, 'I don't give a fuck what people think of me' but I haven't quite gotten there yet. I still have a little ego left that's why I exercise every day and try to be somewhat conscientious of what I say out loud! My mouth can still get me in trouble at times especially around a political discussion but that doesn't stop me when an activist is called for.

From the age of five, I wanted to live on a ranch. I figured (in those days) that I would marry a rancher, but no such luck!

Life throws you curves. It's what you make of those curves that makes you the person you become! No should of, would of, or could of is my motto to live by! Absolutely no regrets! I have lived my life to the fullest, traveled to extraordinary places, met incredible people, and have accomplished most of my bucket list!

I want to leave this planet for my granddaughter in better shape because we can! Shame on the climate deniers and the pussy grabbers! It's up to all of us young and old to do what we can. And if that means protest, you protest!

I believe we are all put on this earth with a purpose. My purpose, of course, was my girls but my other purpose was to bring live theater to my community. It has been my biggest joy to show children my passion of singing, dancing and acting. Not only to my community but now I share my passion with my other community in Costa Rica. Seeing these children *in a foreign country thrive through theater has been an utter delight.*

We all have a story to share. Share it however you can! I decided to write my memoirs for my granddaughter to read when she turns eighteen! How else will our grandchildren know us, our real selves unedited flaws and all! Our stories are our truths. Like it or not!

J.J.

"To never stop searching and know I can do this."

———

I have come to understand that with the loss of youth comes wisdom. I'm OK with my age. It seems it kinda snuck up on me, like, how did this happen so fast? But I do not think about how old I am (only the doctors do)! I like that I am determined to keep on stretching to attract more awareness.

Am I worried about losing my looks, money or marbles? No, I'm really not afraid of aging. My only concern is using my time to evolve my consciousness to an awareness that I am an expression of divinity so that I will wake up knowing that in my next incarnation.

How do I view myself? I am wiser. I feel grateful

for how far I have come from my beginning in this life, having been raised Southern Baptist—from that old fear and guilt-based control to the acceptance of being a spiritual consciousness. Becoming aware of divine perfection (bit by bit) I have learned so much from my experiences and mistakes, what to dismiss, what to accept.

As tempting as it can be to worry about the future, I make a genuine effort to surrender and 'let go' of fearful concerns and trust that the universe has its best plan for me. (Do you want to make God laugh? Tell him your plans! Right?)

Though I am not a fearful person, stuff does surface occasionally and if I am paying attention, I will make an effort to feel it and consciously release it and send it light and love. I just do not want to live to be old and wane slowly. I want to live until I die and transcend when I am done on this earth.

My relationships with family and community are good. I know of no conflicts. It's important to me to be a positive person of integrity and live life with grace. That includes being goofy and having a good time, enjoying fellowship with dear friends and family, and sharing all the experiences, the good and the challenging.

I mean for my legacy to inspire that there is a divinity that vibrates within us all. To never stop searching and always know 'I can do this.' My sincere hope is managing my aging years as an inspiration to each of us so that we may all allow the ascension of Christ Awareness. I am happy now. I enjoy my life even though I have just recently become aware of serious financial concerns (I have to sell my property). I am very determined to manifest a positive outcome. I will be as happy as I choose to be.

Cynthia

"Every age is valuable."

So how do I feel about being a woman of a certain age? Well, it depends on the day. And my mood. And the mirror. And the lighting. And whether I'm camping among a group of full time 'RVers' or visiting friends in the city who dress to kill. It depends on whether I'm sitting in a bar waiting to be waited on by someone who makes me feel invisible or doing yoga with fat, stiff people.

Wisdom. Devil-may-care attitude. Having wonderful memories. Getting to say "I'm seventy-years-old and I don't have to do anything I don't want to do," whether true or not.

Am I scared? Not really, but I've always been an optimist. My mother died of Alzheimer's, and yes, that crosses my mind. I wonder if I get it will I tell my husband or try to hide it like so many women do (and my mother did, I'm sure, as I look back on her actions). I bet I try to hide it. I hide that I sometimes ought to be wearing pads in case I leak. Why wouldn't I hide about losing my mind?

Hmmm, do I place value on age. Yes, absolutely. When we decided to change careers at fifty-two many people told us we were too old. Motor yachting was a young man's job—and they had them all sewed up. We'd never get hired, and could we even do it anyway? Well, I never doubted we were right for the job. We had the intelligence, the experience, the ability to speak to anyone at any level about any subject and make them feel right at home. Young people just can't relate. We could and do. We were the most sought-after crew because of our age. I loved that!!

Every age is valuable though. Each age is a stage and each stage teaches us things that we bring into the next age. Maturity is the key, being the right maturity for your age is the trick. On the other hand, as a seventy-year-old woman I'm sure I'm expected to be a lot of things I'm not! Like old. And boring. And tired of life. And uninterested in trying new things. You could say I'm not dependable like an old person should be always there, always ready to babysit or watch the dog. I've got a lot of life left and I'm living it in spite of my age.

There are seven stages of age—a ninety-plus-year-old man told me this but I can't remember all of them—cause I'm too old! Here's a version that's close: Biological—the condition your organs are in. Physiological—what shape your body is in. Mental—how developed your brain is. Sexual—how experienced you are sexually. Chronological—the number of years old you are. Psychological—how in tune you are with your psyche. Social—who you relate to and how.

My legacy will be the spirit I've instilled in my children and grandchildren. Their imagination for what can be, their belief in themselves, their enthusiasm for life and their love of nature and the ocean make me proud.

(The icing on the cake will be if they, like me, refuse to tolerate the words "I'm bored . . ." and "I hate . . .")

"I'm very happy with my life, at least for this fifteen minutes" as I've been trained to say by my best friend in the world. I'm grateful every day that I have the life I live. It continues to be very adventurous food for my soul.

Susan

"Nowadays, I am so much more tolerant."

———

I certainly don't find aging to be appalling or anything like that. In fact, overall, I like it. I've earned my age and I wear it with distinction. But sometimes I hear the clock ticking so loud, the days going by faster and faster and I have so much I want to do. It's wonderful to still feel excited about what the future might hold, but I feel like my time is running out, and so is my energy to pursue some of those things on my bucket list. A trip to ride a Bactrian Camel on the Mongolian Steppes is probably out, as is climbing Mount Rainier, or singing in a band, or . . . well, you get the picture. I might have a shot at finishing that quilt though, or maybe riding a mule on a camping trip, or even seeing a woman president. A girl can hope.

I think we dance around aging way too much, like it's a bad thing, like we're supposed to be sad that we don't look thirty years old anymore. Hell, I wouldn't go back to twenty, thirty or even forty for anything. I'm wiser, happier and kinder now than I ever was then. I was always so worried about everything: my looks, my finances, my romances, my career, my family. Sure,

I still worry about things, but not so much about how my hair looks, or what someone else thinks about me.

I'm quieter these days than I imagined I would be. Maybe because I am more peaceful? Well, I like to think so.

Now I know how hard life is. People get so very broken. I think accepting people the way they are is the trick, not that it's always easy. But I'm firm in the belief that it is our job to love one another without judging. We can't know what makes someone else tick, or what challenges they've faced, or what heartbreaks they have endured.

Nowadays, I am so much more tolerant of my own, and other's idiosyncrasies. Even when they annoy the crap out of me, I still find them kind of endearing in some sweet, quirky way. After all, there is no one "right" answer for any life. There are just options— some good, some better, none perfect, but all ought to be interesting at least.

Finally, I have to believe there are more best days ahead. Even with life's struggles, it can still be breathtaking and inspiring at times. Life isn't over till it's over and who knows what may happen next? Just because we are aging, is no reason to start playing dead already.

L.A.

"I always enjoyed a little mischief."

———

I was a hairdresser for years which allowed me to choose my own hours. Then I fell into my home-based business, *Chic Skins*, designing leather clothing for a hand full of country stars. Those twenty-five years I can honestly say were the sunshine of my life, I was able to travel, meet interesting people and my clothes were featured in some of the finest boutiques in the country.

I always knew that certain behaviors could age one's self. Therefore, I never smoked cigarettes, used drugs or drank a lot of alcohol. If I drank, it was only in moderation or not at all. Now I don't want to sound like I'm a "goodie 2 shoes;" I always enjoyed a little mischief and good belly laughs!

Even being careless or hasty can cause permanent changes or damage in one's life. I will share some of my careless choices.

I live with my husband, who adores me, on our small Hobby Farm in the heart of the Wine Country. We have horses, chickens, peacocks, indoor and outdoor cats. My husband is an excavator and a very talented builder. He promised I would never be bored *and he was right.*

Through all of the ups and downs we have a lot to be thankful for. One thing we're both thankful for is that we grew up in a time when life was simpler.

I don't like to think about aging, but it sure beats the heck out of the dirt nap!!

Shelly

"I am trying to learn this art of living with sorrow."

———

There is no getting away from the fact that when it comes to grief, attitude is everything and even our grief is what we make it. Life is the original DIY job. The good news and the bad news are all rolled into one.

We widows learn to be tough. What widowed people really experience is losing part of our identity.

I'm OK, my life is moving forward and I am grateful for all of my blessings, but there is such a hole in my life that will never be filled. You just have to learn to live with it. I am trying to learn this art of living with sorrow but right now I don't know if I will ever reach that point. It's like being homesick, even though I am as home now as I ever was, I still feel homeless, like I'm looking in a mirror without a reflection. I miss a future I didn't get to have— existential homesickness.

I miss our inside jokes. I miss being sharp and witty. My mind isn't as quick since Alan died. I think I may have used it up when navigating the medical system. I miss the future we didn't get to have, the adventures and arguments, the decisions and delights.

There are no answers. I am still trying to make sense of it all. What helped me was supportive, caring friends and family, exercise, letting myself cry, my dogs, grief support and therapy, medication, reading, writing, keeping a gratitude journal, square dancing, volunteer work and making new friends. And now I am teaching drawing classes.

Sharon C.

"Listening to our gut . . ."

———

Every age in my opinion has its ups and downs. It's the lens we are choosing to look through, focusing on the moment and not dwelling on the past or the future.

So many wonderful perks come as we age. Retirement brings with it time to spend with family and friends, grandchildren if we are lucky, no more periods, traveling opportunities, financial security and hobbies to explore.

When fear creeps in, it is losing the advantage of all these wonderful things due to illness or dementia. We can't let fear take over because that means we are giving it energy.

Listening to our gut is always the right choice even when it doesn't feel like it. Later, we always look back and understand why things occurred the way they did. It takes guts to listen to your gut!

The happiest days for me, hands down, was giving birth to my two lovely daughters who are my world. The moment of their births has stayed with me all these years and seems like yesterday.

The darkest day in my life was when my oldest daughter had a large bone tumor removed from her skull. Her incision went from ear to ear, fifty-two stitches, and we had to wait thirty days to hear if it was malignant. With a bone tumor, the oncologist has to slice it slowly and keep testing. I was never so elated than to hear it was benign!

Money was very important when I was younger and our daughters were in college. Job loss occurred many times as did out-of-state moves. At this time, we don't have those financial responsibilities anymore and are fortunate to be debt free. Life is good.

Family means everything to me but we don't always

agree on issues, but we are always trying to improve. I feel extremely blessed to have all of us together through thick and thin. We have cruised together out of the country and shared many wonderful memories. I know in my heart God meant for us to share our lives together.

If I had to live my life over again, I wouldn't change a thing. Bad times made me stronger and good times made me feel humble.

Knowing finally who I am and again listening to my inner voice has lead me to this moment. I am ready for the next chapter and with the Lord's help will handle it all with grace and much joy.

Cathy

"Sign me up!"

———

What is life but a bittersweet mix of sadness, heartbreak, wonderment and joy? Research says that dancing improves brain function and reverses the signs of aging. Researchers hope to develop new dances based on fitness programs which have the potential to maximize the anti-aging affects. I love dancing and music!!

Where do I sign up?

Diana C.

"What I Know Now"

———

I know that love is best.

*I know that we must take care of relationships
because all things languish without care.*

*I know that physical activity is key to a thriving old
age.*

I know that intellectual activity is equally important.

*I know that now, as always, Nature is the companion
of my days.*

*I know that we must take care of the nature around
us, or else we will lose it.*

I know that politics matter.

I know that old age or illness will come.

I know that when it's my turn, death will come.

I know that, in the meantime, I thrive with life.

Women of a certain age are too often portrayed as meek, or weak, or like invisible, little mice. I hope that this book has played a role in changing these outdated notions.

As I collected these marvelous, insightful stories and essays, I came to realize that our strength is in knowing who we are and what we bring to the table. We have discovered that our experiences have connected us to the necessities and rewards of living in a way that our younger selves couldn't possibly know.

If I could sum up what these remarkable women have in common, I would have to call it "resilience." No matter what we have faced, collectively or individually, we have learned that "forward" is the only direction worth pursuing.

My hope is that I can embody even the smallest spark of inspiration that these women have so generously shared.

CPSIA information can be obtained
at www.ICGtesting.com
Printed in the USA
LVHW022055160721
692932LV00009B/522

9 781954 396036